In His Presence

In His Presence

A Handbook for Coming into the Presence of God

Kathy Wypij

In His Presence:
A Handbook for Coming into the Presence of God
Available through:
Kathy Wypij Ministries.com
or Amazon.com

Copyright © 2015 Kathy Wypij
All rights reserved.

ISBN: 1519369476
ISBN 13: 9781519369475

Endorsements

"IN THE PAST others have written about the importance of God's presence, but Kathy has given us a fresh, insightful, practical and prophetic call to cultivate the Presence of God in our lives. It is much needed for the times we are living in. Anyone would be enriched and strengthened by reading *In His Presence*."

Pastor Jeff Hokenson, Senior Pastor, Pioneer Christian Fellowship, Arcade, New York

"Need a practical, real world guide to practicing God's presence? Kathy gently takes the reader on a joyous journey, accompanied by the Holy Spirit, into a deeper relationship with the triune God through her book *In His Presence*. This book has the potential to produce life-changing results for any willing soul."

Jodi Hokenson, M.Ed. Author of the *The Well at Ndhiwa*, Elim Fellowship Global Ministries member, Pioneer Christian's MAT leader, and a NYS High School Equivalency Instructor, Arcade, New York

"*In His Presence* is a compelling read for anyone desiring to live in and experience the marvelous presence and power of God. Kathy uses such vivid, real life examples that as a part of her journey illustrate the revelations of His presence of which she writes. Each of us has a key role to fulfill in what God is doing in this generation and the generations that follow. The revelations contained in this book will cause you to shake off doubt and unbelief empowering you to live in His presence and demonstrate His supernatural power. This book will set you ablaze with a zeal for His presence and power!"

Apostle Barbara Burkholder, Co-Director of Christian International of Canada, New York/Ontario Regional Leader for Christian International, and Founder/Co-Pastor of Sword of the Spirit Ministries, Buffalo, New York

"Kathy's book, *In His Presence*, is an insightful read which builds a desire in the heart of the reader to draw close to God's Presence. A longing to come close to the Spirit of God is sparked as Kathy lays out both the way and the benefits of coming into God's Presence. Read on and allow your heart to be touched by His wonderful Presence."

Apostle John W. Bowers, Tri-state Regional Leader for Christian International, Senior Pastor, Grace Fellowship International Church, Erie, Pennsylvania

Contents

Foreword

KATHY WYPIJ HAS blessed the Body of Christ with the greatest insight concerning the Presence of God. She reveals what it takes to appropriate God's presence, and she describes what the presence of God is in character, blessings, and power.

You can depend on the faithfulness of the presence of God. It will enlighten, empower and bless you beyond imagination if you know how to relate to His presence, possess His presence and manifest God's presence. The presence of Jesus Christ will not only bring great peace and joy into our lives but will produce mighty miracles.

The presence of Jesus Christ not only gives protection from evil but also power to overcome and live victorious in Jesus Christ.

Bless you, Kathy, for blessing us with such an understanding of Christ's presence and developing such a hunger for more of His presence.

Kathy Wypij

By: Bishop Bill Hamon
Bishop and Founder of Christian
International Apostolic Network

Author: *The Eternal Church; Prophets & Personal Prophecy; Prophets & the Prophetic Movement; Prophets, Pitfalls, & Principles; Birthing God's Purpose; Fulfilling Your Personal Prophecy; Prophetic Destiny and the Apostolic Movement; Apostles/Prophets & the Coming Moves of God; The Day of the Saints; Who Am I & Why Am I Here?; Prophetic Scriptures Yet to be Fulfilled; 70 Reasons for Speaking in Tongues; and How Can These Things Be?*

Acknowledgements

WRITING THIS BOOK, *In His Presence*, has been an act of obedience that came forth from God's heavenly directive. It is a fruit that has been birthed only from abiding in His daily Presence; therefore, I first of all thank my Lord and Savior Jesus Christ for His Presence in my life that has only been enriched through this book's writing.

Many thanks to my husband, Mike, for his loving support that made it possible for me to write this book. Also, I thank Jodi Hokenson for her editing of the manuscript, for her endorsement, and encouragement. Jodi, you are a blessing! I also want to thank Pastor Jeff Hokenson and Apostles Barbara Burkholder and John Bowers for their love, guidance, and endorsements. Many thanks also to Bishop Bill Hamon for his foreword and leadership. Thank you to my youngest son, Justin, for his beautiful photograph used on the cover of this book. And finally, many thanks to the many intercessors who remembered me in prayer as I went about the Lord's work of writing.

Introduction

To BE IN the presence of royalty is a great honor and privilege for anyone. The royal weddings of England, for example, attracted the attention of the world. Thousands of people flocked to England to watch these grand events. Still others crowded around their television sets in awe of the majesty of the occasion. Those who were invited to these special events were privileged, to say the least, and for those who lived nearby or were vacationing in the area, they were certainly fortunate to be there. If they were close enough to catch a glimpse of the royal couple, they counted themselves blessed indeed to witness the historic royal occasion.

Our God is certainly the "King of Kings, and the Lord of Lords" (Revelation 19:16). It is indeed a privilege to come into His Divine Presence. But are we invited? The answer is an emphatic *Yes*!

In the parable of the wedding banquet, (see Matthew 22:1-14; Luke 14:16-24) the Kingdom of Heaven is likened to a wedding feast. The king sends out invitations for the wedding banquet of his son. Those first invited did not realize the privilege of the invitation. They made excuses for not coming.

One said that they just bought a field and had to go to see it, and another said they just bought five yoke of oxen and had to go to try them out. Still another said that they were recently married and so declined the invitation. All of these things were indeed important, but in the eye of the beholder, they took precedence over their privileged invitation. Their priorities were out of order.

The king in the parable was angry at their lack of respect and poor response. He then opened up the invitation for all to come. He sent word out to the highways and the byways. It was a "come one, come all" invitation. Likewise, our Heavenly King invites us all to come and be a part of His Kingdom and to dwell in His Divine Presence. It is indeed a "come one, come all" invitation.

The question is, "What should be our response?" Will we recognize the daily invitation to come into His Presence? Will we see this invitation as the privilege it is, or will we get caught up in the busyness of life and make excuses? The fact that you are holding this book shows a willingness to accept His invitation and come into His Presence. Read on, my friend, and experience the richness of His goodness and the benefits of His Divine Presence.

My heart is overflowing with a good theme;
I recite my composition concerning the King;
my tongue is the pen of a ready writer.

~ Psalm 45:1 ~

CHAPTER 1

Created to Be in His Presence

But now, thus says the LORD, who created
you, O Jacob,
and He who formed you, O Israel:
"Fear not, for I have redeemed you;
I have called you by your name;
you are Mine."

~ ISAIAH 43:1 ~

GOD HAS ALWAYS wanted to dwell with His highest creation—mankind. His motive for creating us is love. The Holy Trinity—God the Father, Son, and Holy Spirit was complete in and of themselves. However, God desired to pour forth His love. To do so, there had to be a recipient—one to receive His limitless love. Just as parents desire to have children to love, so also God desires to have children to pour out His limitless love upon.

Did you ever notice how children resemble their parents? My husband, Mike, and I have two grown sons, and we can see resemblances in them of ourselves. Our tiny granddaughters also resemble our son and daughter-in-law. As children grow, they pick up our speech and mannerisms. Why is that? God designed it that way. He started it. "Then God said, 'Let Us make man in Our image, according to Our likeness'" (Genesis 1:26a). It is the Trinity speaking here; the Father is speaking with the Son and the Spirit. God had a desire for children made in His image and likeness—children to love and to be with. And so God created mankind, male and female (see Genesis 1:27). We were created in His image and to be in His Presence—to be with Him.

Good parents desire to have their children with them. They desire to spend time with their kids, to watch them grow, to love on them, to have them draw near to them, and to hold them in their arms. God too desires to be with His children. It has been so from the beginning. We see in the third chapter of Genesis that God walked and talked with His children, Adam and Eve, in the Garden in the cool of the day. They conversed with one another. They had a relationship— a close relationship. But something happened—a falling out took place—a breach in the relationship. How did it happen? Just as any break up happens, a transgression occurred. When you suffer a break up in a relationship, it's because there is an offense—a transgression of one against another that results in the falling out of the relationship.

This is how it happened: The woman was deceived into eating the fruit that God had forbidden and she then gave it to her husband and he ate of it also. The forbidden fruit possessed the knowledge of good and evil, therefore, partaking of it brought the instant feeling of guilt and shame for they realized what they did was wrong and also that they were now naked. Their eyes were opened to the reality of what they had done—they had trespassed against God. Therefore, *they hid themselves from the Presence of the Lord* out of shame (see Genesis 3:1-8). A trespass occurred in their relationship with God; it is called sin.

Now, sin did not stop God's love for us. He has never stopped loving us. It did, however, drive a wedge of separation between mankind and our Divine Creator/Father God, and for good reason. You see—sin cannot dwell in the Presence of a Holy God. It is a simple truth—sin separates us from God.

The Separation

Many of you have seen the "Bridge to Life" illustration that shows a person on one side of a deep chasm and God on the other. I shared this illustration from NavPress with permission in the first chapter of my first book, *The Keys to the Kingdom*. The chasm between the two is wider and deeper than anything we could imagine. It is wider than the widest span of the widest canyon and deeper than the deepest sea. It is a vast separation that occurred because of mankind's sinful state. No bridge built by the greatest architect and no work done in man's most sincere efforts can connect God with mankind. No work man or woman could dream up or work up could possibly be able to reach across and mend this vastly wide breach. It all comes up short! That's why the Word of God tells us, "For all have sinned and come short of the glory of God" (Romans 3:23). Our most sincere efforts won't connect us to His Presence. Romans 3:10 tells us that no one is righteous. No one! For we all inherited the "sin gene" so to speak. The Bible also tells us that "the wages of sin is death" (Romans 6:23). In other words, sin pays us back—death.

Now spiritually speaking, the definition of death is more than just to stop breathing someday and to physically die; spiritual death is *separation from God*. To be separated from God (in relationship) is to be spiritually dead. Oh, you live physically, you take in oxygen, you walk around, but you are the walking dead. You may have a job, but your life is spent. You may have money, but you are spiritually bankrupt. And although you may possess the whole world, you have nothing of eternal value.

This great distance we have from God is something people are aware of to one extent or another. People feel like if there is a God, He is out there somewhere, but you can't know Him. They feel the distance. Some are aware of their sinful state and, therefore, feel that they cannot come into God's Presence (much like Adam and Eve felt after the Fall). This is why when invited to church, they say things like, "Oh if I were to come to church, it would probably fall down on me." They are aware of their sin and their state of being separated from God and as a result, they are afraid to draw near to Him.

The bottom line is…our sin is a problem! Nevertheless, God has always wanted to be reunited with His children. He wants to be with us, and He wants us to be near Him. This "sin issue", however, made it impossible. You see, as I stated before, sin cannot dwell in the midst of God. The reason is...God is Holy. That means He is all together pure, righteous, and sinless. Therefore, sin cannot come into His Presence, and if it does, it will be destroyed. And if it happens to be attached to mankind (and it is), then guess what? Poof! Destroyed! That's right, gone! So what I'm saying is...God in His mercy, historically kept a distance, so to speak, and His motive was *LOVE!*

Kept at Bay

It was as though a curtain was drawn between sinful mankind and the holy God to protect us from being utterly destroyed in His Presence. There are some good examples of this found in the Old Testament Scriptures. One good example of God keeping His people at bay out of love is when He called Moses up to Mount Sinai to give him the Ten Commandments:

> Then it came to pass on the third day, in the morning, that there were thunderings and lightnings, and a thick cloud on the mountain; and the sound of the trumpet was very loud, so that all the people who were in the camp trembled. And Moses brought the people out of the camp to meet with God, and they stood at the foot of the mountain. Now Mount Sinai was completely in smoke, because the LORD descended upon it in fire. Its smoke ascended like the smoke of a furnace, and the whole mountain quaked greatly. And when the blast

of the trumpet sounded long and became louder and louder, Moses spoke, and God answered him by voice. Then the LORD came down upon Mount Sinai, on the top of the mountain. And the LORD called Moses to the top of the mountain, and Moses went up.

And the LORD said to Moses, "Go down and warn the people, lest they break through to gaze at the LORD, and many of them perish. Also let the priests who come near the LORD consecrate themselves, lest the LORD break out against them."

But Moses said to the LORD, "The people cannot come up to Mount Sinai; for You warned us, saying, 'Set bounds around the mountain and consecrate it.'"

Then the LORD said to him, "Away! Get down and then come up, you and Aaron with you. But do not let the priests and the people break through to come up to the LORD, lest He break out against them." So Moses went down to the people and spoke to them."

~ Exodus 19:16-25 ~

Notice the Scripture said that even the priest had to be consecrated—that means made holy, prepared, and set apart. And Aaron was chosen to go with Moses. However, we get more details in Exodus chapter 24: "Now He said to Moses, 'Come up to the

LORD, you and Aaron, Nadab and Abihu, and seventy of the elders of Israel, and worship from afar'" (Exodus 24:1). Here we see those who were invited to come at least part way up the mountain of the Lord were actually able to see God (see Exodus 24:9-11). But it was only Moses who could come into God's Presence at that time. Joshua, his assistant, was allowed to assist him up the mountain part way, but only Moses went up to be with God.

So Moses went up to be with God on top of Mount Sinai and the glory of the Lord descended upon the mountain. To the people below God's glory looked like a consuming fire. This is a fitting description since the Scriptures tell us that God is a consuming fire (see Deuteronomy 4:24; Hebrews 12:29). They were afraid to come near that they might be consumed and rightly so! However, Exodus 33:11 tells us that God spoke to Moses face to face, as a friend.

Camping with God

It was during Moses' time upon Mount Sinai with God that he received not only the Ten Commandments, but also the mandate and instructions to construct the Ark of the Covenant, a box that would hold the Ten Commandments, some manna that they were fed by God while traveling in the wilderness, and Aaron's staff that budded miraculously. This Ark of the Covenant is a box where God would place His Presence in a strong way. While upon the Mount, God also instructed Moses about the building of the Tabernacle—a portable tent-like structure that would house this Ark of the Covenant within it.

You may ask, "Why on earth would God place His Presence upon a box and inside a tent?" *Because, He so wanted to dwell with His people!* He wanted to be with them. His heart has always wanted to be with His people! We were created to be in His Presence.

When I was camping with my family one day, the Lord gave me a great revelation of this. It was many years ago when our two sons, Josh and Justin, were little boys. We went to an area campground camping with another family. Our children and my husband were very excited about our adventure. I, however, was less than enthusiastic. Actually, I had adopted quite an attitude. You see, I would rather have been at a nice bed and breakfast or a luxury hotel than camping in a tent. Camping was beneath me. So I was not a "happy camper."

The Lord confronted my bad attitude as I was walking down the camp road on my way to the public shower. It was there on the camp road that I had a type of "Damascus Road" experience. God spoke to me clearly. He said that during the Old Testament time of Moses He so desired to be with His people that *He* was willing to *dwell in a tent* to be near them! Well, this greatly humbled me. My arrogant pride was broken. I literally fell to my knees right there on that camp road. So there I was, on that camp road, surrounded by tents and campers, on my knees weeping before the Lord.

When I returned to our campsite, I shared my revelation with my husband, Mike. He responded, "My prayers have been answered!" I am glad to say that I now am a "happy camper."

(Although, I am also happy to say that in recent years, we up-graded to a pop up camper. Glory to God!)

Temporary Fix

Our loving God humbly dwelt in a mere tent to be near His people! Think of it: The Tabernacle that housed the Ark of His Presence was nothing more than a mere tent! What a loving God we serve! There still was the sin problem, though, and His people still couldn't get too close. To assure that a safe distance was kept, the Lord instructed Moses to have a thick, heavy curtain or veil placed before the Ark of His Presence. This separated the space. The room before the Ark of the Covenant was the Holy Place, and the room that contained the Ark was the Holiest of Holies, or Most Holy Place. No one was allowed behind the veil, but once a year the high priest (who was consecrated) would enter for the purpose of offering up a blood sacrifice of a lamb for both his sins and the sins of the people.

The Israelites were familiar with the idea of the blood sacrifice to cover them for the Passover that the Lord instructed for them to establish. This Passover began as they left Egypt. The Lord told them, through Moses, to slaughter a lamb and place its blood upon the doorpost of their homes. This blood covered them and kept them protected when the death angel "passed over" and killed the first born of the Egyptians in judgment. Also, before Moses went up Mount Sinai, he made sacrifices as the Lord instructed and sprinkled the "blood of the covenant" upon the people (see Exodus 24:5-8). All this was a temporary fix, however, and did not permanently deal with the sin problem. The people were still not granted access into God's Holy Presence.

Although sin was still a problem, nevertheless, God's desire was always to dwell with His people. He only kept them at a distance in order to protect them from being destroyed. That is why when Moses told God that he desired to see God's glory—to get yet closer—God put Moses within the cleft of a rock and said that He would pass by him but would cover Moses with His hand until He passed by. Then He moved His hand so Moses could see His back but not His face for no one could see God's face and live (see Exodus 33:18-23). God spoke to Moses "face to face" as a friend, yet Moses didn't actually *see* His face.

Sin was Still a Problem

There was another account in Scripture, during the time of the Priest Eli, that the Ark of the Covenant was stolen by the Philistines. This was during a time of defeat, for the blessing of God was not upon them as a result of their sin and disobedience. However, the Ark did not bless this enemy of Israel, but rather brought a curse upon them and brought death into their camp, and those who were not killed were struck with tumors. This made them afraid, and they wanted to return the Ark of the Lord to where it belonged. Therefore, they hooked the Ark of the Lord to a newly built cattle-drawn cart with some offerings they had fashioned and let it go. God in His sovereignty brought it back home to His people of Israel and it was found by the people of Beth Shemesh. God's people rejoiced at the return of the Ark of the Lord the Levites had retrieved, and the people offered sacrifices to the Lord. Their rejoicing was cut short, however, when some presumptuous men dared to look into the Ark of the Covenant (which they were forbidden to do), and the Lord struck them down as a result (see 1 Samuel 6:13-19; Numbers 4:20). This again was the result of unconsecrated people coming into contact with a Holy God.

The people of Beth Shemesh were then made much afraid after this great judgment, and so they asked their brothers at Kirjath Jearim to come and take the Ark with them. The people of Kirjath Jearim came and retrieved the Ark of the Covenant and brought it to the home of a godly man named Abinadab. His son Eleazar was consecrated to keep the Ark, and it remained there for twenty years (see 1 Samuel 6:20-21; 7:1-2).

Another time after David was installed as King, when moving the Ark of the Lord to the new capital, Jerusalem, one of Abinadab's sons Uzzah reached out to steady the Ark when it began to fall from its brace that held it up for transport, and he was struck dead for touching it. This may seem harsh, but again it illustrates the reality that sin cannot dwell in the Presence of a Holy God (see 2 Samuel 6:1-11). The fear of the Lord struck King David; he then had the Ark of Presence taken to the house of Obed-Edom temporarily. Later, after he saw that the Ark of God's Presence brought blessing to the home of Obed-Edom, he had it moved to Jerusalem. This successful transition was done with much respect and offerings. King David himself found joy in the Presence of the Lord and danced before the Ark of God's Presence as an act of worship (see 2 Samuel 6:11-19).

Though God desired to have His Presence dwell in the midst of His people, the sin problem still caused there to be a separation. In the temple of Solomon, the Ark of the Lord was kept separate within the room called the Most Holy Place (see 1 Kings 8:1-8). Yet, God so desired to be near His people; He longed to have an "open door policy." He longed for His people to have open access into His Presence—to draw near to Him. He wanted to love on His children.

The sin problem had to be dealt with! So in the fullness of time, God sent His Son—His only begotten Son, Jesus Christ—to be the final sacrifice for our sins. He came to fix the sin problem *forever.*

The book of Revelation calls Jesus the Lamb that was slain from the foundation of the world. In other words, God the Father always intended to send Him. He knew that mankind would blow it and sin and cause separation in the relationship from the very beginning. He always had a plan, a redemptive plan, to save us from eternal death and separation from Him. His plan was always to remedy the sin problem by pouring out His own blood for us.

John the Baptist called Jesus the Lamb of God. Like a slaughtered lamb, Jesus came to die. He came to make a way for you and me to come into the very Presence of God. That is why Jesus is called the "Way" (see John 14:6). And so He, the sinless Son of God, was beaten and scourged for our sin. He was mocked, spat upon, and a crown of thorns was thrust upon His head. He was then nailed to a cross. The Bible tells us, "...He was wounded for our transgressions, He was bruised for our iniquities; the chastisement for our peace was upon Him, and by His stripes we are healed" (Isaiah 53:5). As He hung there, He not only felt the weight of the world's sin upon His shoulders, but that sin caused Him to be separated from God the Father for the first and only time ever. He bore not only the penalty of sin for us, but He also bore the separation from God for us as well. That is why He cried out, "My God, My God why have you forsaken me?" (Matthew 27:46). He was crying out from a place of separation. After that, Jesus said, "It is finished" (see John 19:30). He breathed His last, and gave up His Spirit. The Scriptures tell us that at that moment, the curtain of the temple (the new temple) was torn in two *from top to bottom* (see Matthew 27:51)!

Open Door Policy Will You Enter?

This tearing open of the curtain signified the opening up of the way into God's Holy Presence. Jesus, the Way, opened the way into God's Presence for us. All who come through Jesus, the Way, can now come into His very Presence. Who tore the curtain? God the Father did! It was torn from top to bottom! If man had done it, it would have been torn from the bottom to the top. Also, this curtain was very thick and therefore not easily torn in two by mere human hands.

Jesus Christ, our high priest, entered Heaven itself to appear before God the Father, His own blood making it possible. God now is inviting us to come into His Presence. The way is open. "But Christ came as High Priest of the good things to come, with the greater and more perfect tabernacle not made with hands, that is, not of this creation. Not with the blood of goats and calves, but with His own blood He entered the Most Holy Place once for all, having obtained eternal redemption" (Hebrews 9:11-12).

The way has been opened. No longer do you need to allow sin to keep you at a distance from God. He is calling you into His Presence. The sad truth is, when Moses went up to be with the Lord, the people stood at the bottom of the mountain as instructed, and were not able to see the manifestation of the Lord upon the mountain or hear His voice like Moses did; however, they showed no desire—no longing—to want to be in God's Presence or to hear His voice for they said, "You go near and hear all that the LORD our God may say, and tell us all that the LORD our God says to you, and we will hear and do it" (Deuteronomy 5:27). The Lord remarked that He wished they had such a heart—that is to do whatever He told them to do. However, they did not have such a heart. The question is: Do you have such a heart? Do you long to come into His Presence and do whatever He tells you to do? He wants you near to Him. The blood of Jesus Christ has been poured out for you. Accept His sacrifice that was made on your behalf and come to Him in faith believing. His blood covers your sin and consecrates you. Only you must acknowledge to Him that you are a sinner and ask Him to forgive you and strengthen you to be able to walk free from that sin and in obedience to Him. He will then cleanse away your sins. "'Come now, and let us reason together,' says the LORD, 'Though your sins are like scarlet, they shall be as white as snow; though they are red like crimson, they shall be as wool'" (Isaiah 1:18).

Prayer

Pray with me this simple yet powerful prayer: Lord Jesus, I love You. I believe that you came and died for me in order to save me from my sins. I believe You came to die that I might live for You. You made a way into the very Presence of God for me, since you are the Way. I am sorry for my sins. Please forgive me for them and deliver me from them that I may be free from sin to serve You. I thank You that I can now come into Your Presence. Take me there I pray, and help me to come into Your Presence daily. Thank You, Lord. Amen.

Now bask in His Presence. He is here right now. His Presence is surrounding you. Breathe in His Spirit. Ask Him to fill you. Pour out your heart to Him. Then just be still in His Presence.

"Be still, and know that I am God..." Psalm 46:10.

In His Presence is where you are called to be, for you were *created to be in His Presence.*

CHAPTER 2

The Protocol of Entering
His Presence

Enter into His gates with thanksgiving,
and into His courts with praise.
Be thankful to Him, and bless His name.

~ PSALM 100:4 ~

WE WORSHIP THE King of Kings! Just as there is a proper protocol necessary to come before a king or queen, so too, there is a proper protocol required to come into the divine Presence of our Lord. I am a real I *Love Lucy* fan. She is my comic relief to life. I have been watching her episodes for years. One year for Christmas, my husband bought me the entire collection of *I Love Lucy* episodes so I can watch them whenever I want. There are many lessons we can learn from Lucy; although, most of them are lessons of what *not* to do rather than what we should do. She was always getting herself into some hilarious predicament. There is one episode I have watched over and over again, where Lucy was in England and getting ready to meet the Queen. She practiced curtsying until she became stuck in that position! Lucy worked her unique predicament out to her advantage. Since she was stuck in the curtsy, she had some men carry her in and place her before the Queen's presence. It was hilarious!

The Lord does not require us to practice the curtsy; nevertheless, there is a proper protocol necessary in order to come into His Presence. It is a position of the humble and thankful heart that gains us access into the Presence of the Almighty. It is as we humble ourselves before Him that He, in turn, lifts us up (see James 4:10). Just like Lucy was then carried into the presence of the Queen while in her bowed state, this position also will carry us into the Presence of the Almighty! This position of reverence unto God needs to be held onto throughout our daily lives. We may become so consumed with worship of Him that at times we find ourselves literally bowing down to Him.

There is a protocol for coming into His Presence. The Scripture says to "enter into His gates with thanksgiving and into His courts with praise..." (Psalm 100:4). We should not be barging into the throne room with our prayer list, but must remember to take a humble, respectful position when approaching our Lord and King.

The way the television character Lucy got stuck in her curtsy was by practicing that position. We also can get stuck in a position that we practice. Sometimes we get stuck in grumbling and complaining like the Israelites did when wandering through the wilderness. What we practice will set in our lives and character. It makes me think of another television movie—*The Wizard of Oz*. The Tin Man became stuck as well. Dorothy and her companions oiled him up with an old oil can. Oil has the ability to loosen things up when they get stuck. It is the same way with us. As we find ourselves stuck in a bad mood—a poor position—we can call upon the Presence of the Holy Spirit to come and free us up from our negative stance. One of the symbols of the Holy Spirit is oil. We need a fresh oil anointing upon our lives to get us freed up and responsive to His Spirit's Presence. Do you need an adjustment? If so, then bow your heart to Him in surrender and allow the Spirit of God to reposition you in Him. As we take a humble stance, we find ourselves in position to be received by His Majesty. As we surrender our bad attitudes to Him, He adjusts our perspective in life. To come into His Presence, we need to take a humble position. Instead of getting stuck in a bad attitude, let us rather get stuck in a position of humility and respect for His Presence. Doing so will carry us into the presence of royalty.

Coming before the Lord with a grateful heart of thanksgiving will surely get His attention. There are so many things we can thank God for if we stop and think of them. Having a thankful heart and finding things to thank God for throughout our day is a sure way of correcting poor posture. Our new, humble and thankful position will gain us access into the Presence of our King. This attitude helps us to cultivate His Presence in our hearts and lives. We become a joy for others to be around, and our attitude will change the atmosphere around us from one of negativity to one of faith and thanksgiving. This will help others to take that same position. We can lead by example by holding the proper attitude.

"Enter into His gates with thanksgiving, and into His courts with praise. Be thankful to Him, and bless His name" (Psalm 100:4). As we bow our hearts to Him, He leans forward eagerly to welcome us. He welcomes us into His Presence.

The Golden Scepter

You may ask yourself, "Who am I to come into the Lord's Presence?" You may feel unworthy and undeserving. However, our heavenly King is one who desires our presence in His courts. He is inviting us to come.

During the reign of King Ahasuerus in the Old Testament, the people of Israel's very existence was being threatened by the decree that Haman, the king's evil assistant, manipulated the king to write and proclaim throughout the land. The king's own queen, Esther, who was Hebrew, knew that she may have been called into this position of queen for "such a time as this" to go before the king and petition the release of her people Israel. The queen knew that the law forbad anyone to enter the king's presence without being invited; therefore, her very life was at risk with her advance. However, if the king were to hold out his golden scepter to her, her life would be spared. Queen Esther prepared herself with fasting and prayer. She also had other people fast for her. After doing so, she humbly and respectfully approached the king's court before he held out his golden scepter to her. She approached and touched the top of his scepter. In this miraculous meeting, she was received by him and told that she could have whatever she desired, even up to half of the kingdom! (See Esther 3-5:3.)

Because of the sacrificial blood of Jesus on our behalf, the way is opened up to come into God's Divine Presence. He is, in fact, holding out His golden scepter to us. By accepting His death and resurrection in your place, you too are taking hold of the divine scepter; your eyes are meeting with the King of Kings. The death sentence that would have been against you in your approach is now made null and void. You are now free to come into His Presence and to present your petitions. The golden scepter represents God's favor towards us. He looks favorably upon us when we draw near to Him. Because of the blood of Jesus, He no longer sees the sin of the repented saint, but He now sees our faith in Him. His ear is now turned towards us, and His attention is on us. Bow your heart before Him and come into His Divine Presence. The blood of the Lamb has been poured out for you, leading the way into the Presence of the King of Kings. Come into His Presence.

Opening Our Treasures To Him

At the time of Christ the King's birth, men known as magi sought His Presence to pay Him homage. These three kings, as tradition calls them, sought to bring honor and praise to the greatest King. They brought gold, frankincense, and myrrh. The Bible tells us that they opened their treasure to Him and bowed before Him to worship Him (see Matthew 2:11). Likewise, we humbly bow before His Presence and give Him what we hold dear. In actuality, all we have belongs to Him. To hold anything in greater regard than Him, is in fact idolatry. The second commandment tells us to have no other gods before Him (see Exodus 20:3).

In order to keep our treasure from becoming our god, we must keep it surrendered to Him. Daily laying the treasure of our hearts and even our hearts' desires before Him keeps our hearts truly poised towards Him. This fresh surrender of all we have is what keeps our priorities right in life. He must be first before spouse, before children, before vocation, before material possessions, before hopes, before dreams, before *all*. This can be done by dedicating these people and things to Him, as our treasures, giving Him all we have. This is a high form of worship.

God blesses us with children as a gift. When we have children, we give them back to the Lord in a dedication service. This is when we formally surrender our children to Him as our gifts to the Lord. They are our treasures. It is only fitting to give our treasure to the Lord. When we dedicate our children to Him, we are saying, "Lord, they are Yours and I will raise them to serve You and to honor You." This is pleasing to Him. Giving God what we hold dear to our hearts is clearly an act of worship. However, we sometimes take back our treasures without realizing it. It is easy to have your priorities shift unknowingly. Therefore, *daily* opening your treasure to Him is a continual surrender and *rededication* of all you have to Him. As you pray for your children, rededicate them to Him. Even adult children can be declared as the Lord's in the spirit as you pray for their spiritual destinies to be fulfilled.

Casting Our Crowns

In the book of Revelation, the Apostle John writes of his experience in the spirit when the door of Heaven was opened unto him. He saw the Lord upon His throne and the beauty that surrounded Him. He beheld beautiful creatures who worshiped Him and He saw elders, twenty-four in number, who sat upon thrones. They were honored with amazing gold crowns upon their heads. As praise to God was brought forth by the living creatures, the twenty-four elders fell down before Him, "and cast their crowns before the throne, saying:

You are worthy, O LORD,
to receive glory and honor and power;
for You created all things,
and by Your will they exist and were created.

~ REVELATION 4:10-11 ~

This heavenly happening provides the spirit and atmosphere in which we are to come before Him with hearts full of worship, unashamedly bowing ourselves before His Holy Presence, consumed with Him, casting our crowns—all He has bestowed upon us—before Him. All we have belongs to Him. He is worthy of our honor and our praise. His Presence is awe-striking. As we come into His Presence, Heaven surrounds us;

we see things differently because we see them as He sees them. We behold His beauty—His glory.

Bow before Him now; cast your crowns before Him. Bow your heart to Him in sweet surrender. Lay before Him all you hold dear. His Presence is surrounding you and filling you. He is washing away all your concerns. Your worship is pleasing to Him and is drawing Him to you.

The Alabaster Box

In the New Testament we find a woman who approached Jesus with an amazing gift—an alabaster box filled with precious oil. Her name was Mary, and the Scriptures tell us that she approached Jesus and broke open this expensive gift and poured its contents over Jesus' head (see Matthew 26:6-13). She also poured it forth on His feet, anointing them and then wiping them with her hair (see John 12:3). This precious oil was worth three hundred denarius (approximately a year's wages). The disciples criticized this woman saying that the oil could have been sold and the money given to the poor, yet Jesus defended her for He saw her heart of worship. He said that her actions were done to prepare Him for His burial and that she would be remembered and even memorialized for her act of faith (see Matthew 26:12-13).

This woman gave her life's savings in honor and dedication to her beloved Jesus. Even at the risk of being misunderstood and criticized by others, she stepped out and gave Him all she had. Our worship too may be misunderstood. The giving up of our time, money, and our treasures—what we hold dear to us—may be seen by others as a "waste." They may argue that we are wasting our time and resources, or that we should be using our time and resources differently. Jesus, however, sees our *hearts*. He sees when we are giving out of love for Him and this so blesses Him. He also sees insincere actions that may be made to look good to others, and this displeases Him. When we pour out our souls to Him in sincere worship, giving Him our all— His heart is truly moved.

Jesus said that Mary performed this worshipful act in anticipation of His death. In those days, bodies were anointed with fragrant oil after they died. Mary's act was, in fact, a prophetic gesture (though she may have not fully understood it) in signifying Christ's soon to be death and burial on our behalf. Likewise, we may not always fully understand the impact of our worship. We may not always know what effects it may have on us or how it may affect others who may be watching us. However, when we worship Him in spirit and in truth, we do make an impact on everyone involved: God, ourselves, and anyone who may happen to be watching. True worship pushes past any fear of being misunderstood or judged wrongly by others; it does not draw back out of fear of man, but in loving faith approaches God out of a sincere heart. Give your all to Him. He is worthy!

The Protocol of Sanctification

King David realized after the first unsuccessful attempt of retrieving the Ark of God's Presence, that they failed to inquire of the Lord as of the proper order or protocol of retrieving it (see 1 Chronicles 15:11-13). He called forth the priest and Levites as they were the ones appointed by God to carry the

Ark. However, even they needed to be sanctified. Since they did not sanctify themselves the first time nor did they consult with the Lord about His order, He broke out against them.

God calls us to live holy lives. That is what sanctify means—to make holy, set apart. In Old Testament days, animal sacrifices were offered up. Today, we are under the New Covenant of God's grace. This means the final sacrifice has been made—Jesus Christ, the Lamb of God. His blood, however, must be *applied* to our hearts and lives. This is done by faith. Our salvation is obtained by accepting His blood sacrifice as payment for our sin. We then live our lives for Him, because we were bought back from the bondage of sin. We were rescued by the Great Savior; therefore, we now put away all the sin that would hold us back—we cast it off—and follow in His footsteps. We become holy when we are wholly His! Out of our great appreciation for what He has done for us, we surrender all our idols, or false gods—the things we want for pleasure in His place. We now turn them in—make a trade— for the joy of His Presence. In doing so, He walks with us and talks with us and in that sense Eden is restored! We now can walk with Him in the cool of the day, as it was in the beginning (see Genesis 3:8).

Eden comes from a Hebrew word meaning pleasure or delight. When sin is no longer an issue, we are a delight to God and He is a delight to us. We are in pleasure while in His Presence and we, in turn, are His greatest pleasure. When Eden is restored in this way, relationship with God is restored. We now can walk and talk with God as Adam and Eve did in the beginning. We can walk with God as Enoch walked faithfully with Him (see Genesis 5:22-24). There is no greater pleasure than to be in His Presence!

Because we are flesh and blood, we live in a fallen world, and because we are not perfect, we will commit sins of weakness. That means there are times when we will miss the mark. This is no excuse to do so, only a fact that happens. When this occurs, we find ourselves once again at distance from the Lord, not in position (we are still His son or daughter) but in relationship. Think of sin as an offense. When we offend someone, we need to make up with them; we need to tell them that we are sorry and that we will try not to do it again. Our relationship with God is no different; He is a person and has feelings too! We also must come to Him and tell Him that we are sorry, ask for Him to forgive us, and to give us the grace and strength so as not to repeat the offense. "If we say that we have no sin, we deceive ourselves, and the truth is not in us. If we confess our sins, He is faithful and just to forgive us our sins and to cleanse us from all unrighteousness" (1 John 1:8-9).

Remember when you were a child and your mother told you to wash your hands before dinner? She would remind you to wash behind your ears too! If you got dirty from playing outside, your mom or dad would tell you to clean up and change your clothes for dinner. Well, our heavenly Father reminds us that we need to be spiritually clean to come and dine with Him as well. And He has made provision for our cleanliness. He clothes us with robes of righteousness that are spotless and white. The Bible tells us that He is coming for a bride without spot or wrinkle (see Ephesians 5:26-27). In the natural, I usually avoid wearing white because I am always getting it dirty before the day is half over. However, spiritually I also am barely out of bed in the morning and I have soiled my righteous robes with the spot of sin. I have to change my clothes, so to speak. This is done by surrendering it to the Lord and asking Him to change me. He will take off our soiled garment as we repent of it and will give us a fresh clean robe of righteousness. He is faithful and just; the Scripture tells that he cleanses us from all unrighteousness (see 1 John 1:8-9). The Holy Spirit convicts our hearts of sin so we will repent of it and ask Him for forgiveness. It is sad, but many people hide themselves from God out of the shame of sin like Adam and Eve did in the Garden. Oh, my friends, do not hide. Our God is a loving Father who is waiting with arms open wide to receive you to Himself, no matter what you have done. There is no spot of sin that the blood of Christ cannot remove. He is like launderers' soap:

But who can endure the day of His coming?
And who can stand when He appears?
For He is like a refiner's fire
and like launderers' soap.

~ MALACHI 3:2 ~

Think of life as a garden—the Garden of Eden specifically; yes, temptations exist, but so does the Presence of God. Like weeds in a garden sickness, pain, and evil exist, yet His Presence and His power are present to pull up any ungodly growth that has taken root in our lives. And as the old hymn "Great is Thy Faithfulness" says, God gives us "His own dear Presence to cheer and to guide." Live a life set apart for Him. Keep yourself for Him, to be His pleasure and His delight. Walk with God; He is holding out His hand to you now and saying, "Come, My child, and walk with Me." Take His hand.

Display of Delight

King David inquired of the Lord as to His will in regards to his defeat of the Philistines (see 1 Chronicles 14:8-17). He did not presume how and when to go up to defeat them, but instead he inquired of the Lord, and the Lord gave him precise instructions. "Therefore, David inquired again of God, and God said to him, 'You shall not go up after them; circle around them, and come upon them in front of the mulberry trees. And it shall be, when you hear a sound of marching in the tops of the mulberry trees, then you shall go out to battle, for God has gone out before you to strike the camp of the Philistines.' So David did as God commanded him, and they drove back the army of the Philistines from Gibeon as far as Gezer. Then the fame of David went out into all lands, and the LORD brought the fear of him upon all nations" (1 Chronicles 14:14-17).

David learned that if he sought the Lord, he would get strategies and instructions for success. Likewise, David learned that the reason the Lord broke out against them in their first attempt of retrieving the Ark of the Covenant was because they did not seek Him for His instructions on how He desired it to be done. Now, David sought the Lord. He prepared a tent to house the Ark of the Lord in the City of David. He called for the Levites and he gathered all of Israel at Jerusalem to prepare for the return of the Ark. David explained to the people that only the Levites were chosen by God to carry the Ark of God; it was important for them to sanctify themselves. So the Levites sanctified themselves. Ranks of musical leaders were chosen to lead a procession of praise and worship with song and musical instruments before the Ark of the Lord as it journeyed to Jerusalem. " So David, the elders of Israel, and the captains over thousands went to bring up the ark of the covenant of the LORD from the house of Obed-Edom with joy" (1 Chronicles 15:25). Sacrifices of oxen and fattened sheep were also made after those carrying the Ark had gone six paces (see 2 Samuel 6:13). Shouts of joy and trumpet blast were made to commemorate this festive event.

As this festive procession continued, King David, full of joy, broke out in a dance of praise and worship before the Ark of the Lord (see 1 Chronicles 15:25, 29)! This king of Israel, who was to be honored by others for his position of rank and royalty, humbled himself by honoring the King of Kings in this public procession of receiving the Ark of God's Presence! What motivated this triumphant dance? Quite simply ... joy.

King David was so filled with joy that he literally broke out into a dance displaying his overflow of delight! "Delight yourself also in the LORD, and He shall give you the desires of your heart" (Psalms 37:4). When we delight ourselves in the Lord, He, in turn, delights in us! His Presence gives us a reason to dance—a reason to rejoice!

Free to Worship Him

Just as we saw earlier in our New Testament example of the woman with the alabaster box who was misunderstood by some in her display of delightful dedication to the Lord Jesus, so also King David was misunderstood. His very own wife Michal was looking through a window as the procession entered Jerusalem and when she saw her husband, the King, playing music and dancing with all his might, she despised him in her heart (see 1 Chronicles 15:29).

Our praise to the Lord Jesus needs to be one of internal love and devotion to Him. We can honor and praise Him within our hearts continually. God sees our hearts, so He knows the attitude that we are holding. If we are continually holding our hearts poised towards Him and giving Him thanks and praise within our hearts, He sees that and is blessed. However, we also are to praise Him with our mouths. "Therefore by Him let us continually offer the sacrifice of praise to God, that is, the fruit of our lips, giving thanks to His name" (Hebrews 13:15). This is a proper protocol to proceed into His Presence.

Like King David and the woman with the alabaster box, we also must have such a dedicated heart of worship that we are willing to offer public displays of praise and thanksgiving *openly* before the Lord—unashamedly. Such a heart is so filled with praise unto the Lord that the fear of being misunderstood is virtually non-existent. This is a good goal to have in praising our Lord and Savior. If allowed, the fear of what others think will cripple our outward expressions of praise. While it is true that God sees your inward praise of the heart, yet He also delights when we unashamedly break out of the restrictions of reserved behavior and give Him our *all* without fear of being criticized for doing so. I might also add: He is even more delighted when we break out into open expressions of thanks and praise *despite* the inner fear of doing so. We all have felt the self-conscious dread of what others are thinking about us if we pray out loud or praise Him openly. The Bible tells us that the fear of man is a snare (see Proverbs 29:25). A snare is a trap. When we allow our fear to keep us from stepping out in faith, praise, and honor of God, we are trapped. We are trapped by fear; it holds us in its grasp and we are frozen—restricted from doing what our hearts so desire—to magnify the Lord. Rather, we must break free from this fear—this shame of what others will think—and be free to worship Him in spirit and in truth. King David did not care that his wife despised, mocked, and taunted him. He worshiped freely and openly; he humbled himself and even took off his kingly robes to worship the Lord openly and humbly. When his wife ridiculed him and warned of what the maidservants would think, David advised her that his praise was before the Lord and then he answered her by saying, "And I will be even more undignified than this, and will be humble in my own sight. But as for the maidservants of whom you have spoken, by them I will be held in honor" (2 Samuel 6:22). The Bible tells us that on that day King David, who was also a Psalmist, delivered a song of thanksgiving. Most of the contents of this song later became known as Psalm 105. David was unashamed and his outward release of praise not only blessed the Lord but others as well, and we are still receiving the benefits of that praise (see 1 Chronicles 16:7-23; and Psalm 105:1-15). But as for Michal … the Bible tells us that she was judged by the Lord for despising King David's expression of praise and had no children from that day onward (see 2 Samuel 6:23).

Proper protocol will bring us into the Lord's Presence. An acceptance of Christ's shed blood that covers our sins, a heart of sincere, daily, and continual repentance, a request for His sanctification, a heart of worship, a surrender of all we hold dear, a mouth that declares thanksgiving and praise, and a tenacious spirit that is determined to thank and praise Him even publicly when the time arises will surely delight the Lord and bring you into His Presence.

Oh, give thanks to the LORD!
Call upon His name;
make known His deeds among the peoples!
Sing to Him, sing psalms to Him;

talk of all His wondrous works!
Glory in His holy name;
let the hearts of those rejoice who seek
the LORD!

~ Psalm 105:1-3 ~

Prayer

Lord, I humble myself before You. Come, Holy Spirit, and adjust my attitude into a spirit of delightful praise unto You. Forgive me for every high and lofty thought that has repelled Your Presence. I bow my heart before You. I surrender all my treasure to You, for all I have is Yours. Make me holy and clean before You. I praise You and thank You for all You have ever given me. I delight in You! Come, Holy Spirit, and let Your Presence rest upon me I pray. Amen.

Now just bask in His Presence. Let go of all your cares and concerns. Let His Spirit fill and surround you. He is present. He will never leave you nor forsake you. You need only to call upon Him, and He will make His Presence known.

Deep calls unto deep at the noise of Your
waterfalls;
all Your waves and billows have gone over me.

~ Psalm 42:7 ~

CHAPTER 3

Peace in His Presence

Come to Me, all you who labor and are heavy
laden, and I will give you rest.

~ MATTHEW 11:28 ~

ONE OF MY favorite places to go is our family lake house. The
lake there is very still. The water looks like glass. I love to
sit by the shore and watch the reflection in the water. It is so
peaceful and relaxing there. It also is a place where I go to be
alone with the Lord. As Psalm 23 says, "He leads me beside
the still waters. He restores my soul" (Psalm 23:2-3). For me to
enjoy this beautiful location, I have to be willing to take the
time to get into my car and drive up there. Likewise, for us to
enjoy the peace and rest that God has for our souls, we need to
separate ourselves from the busyness of the world and get away
with Him. Jesus is calling us to come unto Him and find rest
for our souls. Jesus would call His disciples to come away with
Him and rest for a while (see Mark 6:31). We have to separate
ourselves from the pressures of the world and get alone with
Him. When we come to Jesus, we receive His peace. How do

we get there? How do you get to that place in Him? That, my friends, is the topic of this whole book: how to come into His Presence.

When I was a child and had to attend school, I really didn't want to be there. I would rather be at home playing with my Siamese kitty cat. Sometimes I would daydream about being there—at home with my kitten. I was in school, but in my thoughts I was at home with my kitty. Of course, the teacher didn't always appreciate my lack of attention; nevertheless, I was where I wanted to be—in thought.

Our thoughts can take us places—good places and bad places. When we think about the Lord and His Presence, we are with Him in our thoughts. Did you ever see someone with a preoccupied look on their face and you asked them, "Where are you?" I have actually had that happen to me before when I was with the Lord in my thoughts. It was clear to those around me that I was elsewhere—somewhere wonderful. Yes, I was; I was with the Lord. Of course, we have to keep our mind on what we are doing also, especially when driving or working, but if you are going to go somewhere in your mind, why not go to be with the Lord? We never need an appointment to be with Him. He is always waiting for us. He longs for us to come away with Him. "Rise up, my love, my fair one, and come away" (Song of Solomon 2:10).

I have had different occupations in my life. Some of them required doing a job where I could have my thoughts to myself. Other jobs were extremely cognitive and required my every thought on my work. I really liked the job where I could have my thoughts to myself more that way I was free to praise Him in my thoughts and silently pray and think upon Him more. However, the job that required my every thought was very stressful. I was thankful for the break time that was every two hours. During break time, I could pray and read my Bible. I also had Scripture verses on my computer where I could read them and pray here and there. The thing is to use your time wisely and be with Him in your thoughts as much as possible. It is about thinking on good and heavenly things—godly things and most of all—*Him*. Apostle Paul said, "Finally, brethren, whatever things are true, whatever things are noble, whatever things are just, whatever things are pure, whatever things are lovely, whatever things are of good report, if there is any virtue and if there is anything praiseworthy—meditate on these things. The things which you learned and received and heard and saw in me, these do, and the God of peace will be with you" (Philippians 4:8-9). Notice, as we think on heavenly things, the God of peace is with us! His peace flows through us as we think on Him, His Word, and His ways.

I have had times when God's Presence and peace fell on me like a cloud. Sometimes this happens at church, but other times while at home or work. We go to church to be with Him, to worship Him, and to be with the body of believers, but He will show up anywhere, we need only to call upon Him. When He shows up, His peace flows like a river through us. He truly does lead us beside the still waters. His Spirit comforts us when we are grieved, and He consoles us when we are troubled. When we are "heavy laden" with the demands of our daily life, He brings rest to our souls.

Peace Robber

Daily life can be filled with things that are designed to rob you of your peace. The cares of this life can take hold of us, if we let them. The medical field has a name for this—anxiety. It seems like more and more people are struggling with anxiety on a daily basis. I used to struggle with it as well. Anxiety will weigh you down, and it will take you over if you allow it. It can entrap you into a life of fear and trepidation. "Anxiety in the heart of man causes depression, But a good word makes it glad" (Proverbs 12:25). This Scripture tells us that anxiety can open the door to depression as well. Depression can overshadow you like a dark cloud and follow your every move. Depression is an overwhelming sadness that robs you of your peace and joy in the Lord. Anxiety is actually a fear that involves taking the cares of the world upon your shoulders. The Hebrew word for anxiety in Proverbs 12:25 means fear, care, heaviness and anxiety. The Bible tells us that we are not to take the care but rather to cast our burdens upon the Lord. "Cast your burden on the LORD, and He shall sustain you; He shall never permit the righteous to be moved" (Psalm 55:22). The world and its troubles can shake you up, but God's Presence brings peace into your heart and calms your fears. God has big shoulders; He can handle the cares of the world. You, however, were not built to carry them. Give them to Him.

I used to be a bit like Martha in the Bible who was anxious and worried about many things (see Luke 10:41). Sometimes our minds just get spinning. "What do I do if this happens? And what if that happens?" We can get all wrapped up in trying to solve problems that haven't even happened yet and probably never will. My oldest son always says that we try to find solutions for things that aren't even problems yet. This is a trap of the enemy. He loves to get the saints all wrapped up in the "What ifs" of life. "What if this happens, and what if that happens." Before you know it, you are a worried wreck! If this lifestyle continues you are headed for a straight up panic attack. Then it's off to the doctor to get medicated. I am not saying that your body may not need a medication, but much of this can be avoided if we simply learn to calm our thoughts and cast our cares upon the Lord.

For years my husband, Mike, would respond to all my anxious concerns with, "I don't care." I thought he was being irresponsible for not caring. Then one day I had lunch with a good pastor friend of mine. She explained that when we get all worked up about things in life and lay awake at night worrying about things, we simply need to find *a different way to process our thoughts.* She said that she had to do this too, and now she changed her thought to "I don't care." At first I was shocked by her response. I told her that my husband tells me that all the time, but I wouldn't listen to him. Somehow when it came from my pastor and mentor friend, I could consider it and then receive it. At first, I thought, "Is that Scriptural?" Then the Lord brought this verse to me, "Casting all your care upon Him, for He cares for you" (1 Peter 5:7). I never saw this verse in that light before. I always knew that Scripture taught us to cast our cares upon the Lord, but what I failed to see was that "He cares for you." Think of it, He cares for you. Not just that he cares about you and takes care of you, although that is true, but also that he cares for you in the sense that He cares so you don't have to! I was finally set free! Now, when worries and fears come my way (and they do), I tell myself, "I don't care! I don't care because He cares for me!" He is the one doing the caring—working out all the details, etc. Now I am not saying to be irresponsible in life, but let's face it, if you are prone to anxious thoughts, you worry about things. And as my youngest son pointed out, this is actually sin, because then we are not trusting in God. He desires to bring His peace into your life, and deliver you out of the vicious cycle of fear and anxiety. "Be anxious for nothing, but in everything by prayer and supplication, with thanksgiving, let your requests be made known to God; and the peace of God, which surpasses all understanding, will guard your hearts and minds through Christ Jesus" (Philippians 4:6-7). Rather than worrying about something, pray about it instead, and then give it to God. He will do the caring for you. Then begin to praise Him, remember … praise brings you into His Presence and His peace comes with Him. I thank and praise Him that He set me free from anxiety! Come into His Presence, and He will bring you His peace as well.

Peace in the Midst of the Storm

My husband and I are avid kayakers. There are barely any bodies of water in our area that we haven't paddled in. One time we were on a getaway to Canada staying at a beach where there is camping right along Lake Erie. We put our boats in and started along the coastline with a destination in mind. The weather was fine when we launched out but, suddenly, the wind picked up and the clouds rolled in. Before we knew it, thunder and lightning were striking all around us! We were already quite a ways out, and there was no place to pull into. Marshes were all along the shore. We ended up taking cover in the marshes and lying down low in our boats during the lightning strikes and paddling in between strikes. I was praying fervently and even rebuking the storm in Jesus' name. The ironic part of the whole thing is I was reading the Scriptures about Jesus calming the storm in preparation for writing this chapter earlier that same morning! I guess the Lord thought I needed a real life experience to exercise my faith and write about! Well we made it back all right; the Lord was *with us*. Glory to His Name!

That is how life is. We are busy doing life, when *suddenly* we find ourselves in the midst of a storm. Not only that but it happens when we are following Him! The account of the disciples getting caught in a storm while in a boat starts out by saying that Jesus got into the boat *first*, they then followed Him there (see Matthew 8:23). It then goes on to say that the storm came about *suddenly*. Many times that is how it is for us as well; we believe we are following Jesus into a new adventure when suddenly a storm surrounds us. It is then that the doubts and fears arise—"But God, I thought You were leading me." And, "Where are You God? Don't You care?" That is exactly what the disciples did. The disciples asked, "Teacher, do You not care that we are perishing?" (Mark 4:38). The storm, however, is designed to test our faith. It is during the storms of life that we find out what we are made of.

The interesting thing about Jesus is He was sleeping during the storm. Jesus was at perfect peace because He is perfect peace. The rocking of the boat did not rock His faith because He is the Rock of our faith! The waves did not overwhelm Him because He overwhelms the waves of life. The thing for us to remember during the storms of life is He is in the boat *with us*. He is *with us!* The Bible tells us that He will never leave us nor forsake us (see Hebrews 13:5). We tend to forget that He is with us. This is because we tend to be moved by our emotions. We are an emotional people. We have feelings of fear that can come upon us *suddenly*, like the circumstances that accompany them. It is then that we have a choice. Are we going to allow these fears to overcome our faith? Are we going to be overwhelmed by the waves of life, or are we going to remember that Jesus is in the boat with us?

He hasn't left you. No matter how scary life is for you right now, remember He is in the boat with you, and that makes it a lifeboat, because Jesus saves! You are in the lifeboat with Jesus. "Do not be afraid of sudden terror, nor of trouble from the wicked when it comes; for the LORD will be your confidence ..." (Proverbs 3:25-26).

Remembering that He is *with us* is the first step in experiencing His Presence in the midst of the storm. Even when we don't *feel* Him, if we remember theologically that He is with us, this in and of itself fights off the doubt and unbelief that wants to attack us. No matter how bad it gets, remember that He is with you. "When you pass through the waters, I will be with you; and through the rivers, they shall not overflow you ..." (Isaiah 43:2). Though the disciples were overcome with fear, they had one thing going for them: they *remembered* that

Jesus was with them. They then went to the stern of the boat where they found Him asleep on a pillow (see Mark 4:38). The stern is the aft or back of the boat and this is where they found Him. In a similar way, we have in the back of our minds somewhere the knowledge that Jesus is with us, we must simply visit that thought. When we remember that He is with us, we then can call upon His Presence. "He shall call upon Me, and I will answer him; I will be with him in trouble; I will deliver him and honor him" (Psalm 91:15).

After remembering His Presence we can then call upon the Name of the Lord in faith believing that He is with us. We can call upon Him for wisdom and strategy of what to do in the midst of the storm. The Scripture says that after the disciples called upon Him, He *arose*. He will arise in your life. Even now, as you call upon Him, His Presence is there with you. We see in this Scriptural account when the disciples called Him, He *arose*! He shall arise in your life. He will make His Presence known. Your faith is what stirs Him into action. He arises with healing in His wings (see Malachi 4:2). Even now, His Spirit is stirring within you. His Spirit is hovering over you as it did on the first day of creation—waiting for the Word of God to be spoken so faith is released into action (see Genesis 1). When in the boat with the disciples, Jesus arose and rebuked the wind. You are His body (see 1 Corinthians 12:27). Speak out His word against the winds of adversity in your life. Speak out His Spirit-filled Words of faith that arise within your soul. He arises, and so does His Word. His Word arises so you will speak it out. Declare His Word and take authority over the torrents of adversity. He truly does watch over His Word to perform it (see Jeremiah 1:12).

Peace Be Still

> Then He arose and rebuked the wind, and said to the sea, 'Peace, be still!' And the wind ceased and there was a great calm.
>
> ~ MARK 4:39 ~

When Jesus arose and rebuked the wind, He said, "Peace, be still." The storm obeyed His command! Jesus' influence over even the natural elements spoke magnitudes of His authority. The wind and waves settled down at His command and a great calm came.

Jesus still speaks to the storms of our lives. We all want the calm, but the truth is there are storms in this life. Jesus speaks calm into our hearts and lives. His Words bring comfort and peace in the midst of our storms. The next time a storm arises in your life, look to Him and His Word for what He says on the topic. His Word is still speaking. Is the storm in your life health related? Are your finances being buffeted by the winds of change? Are relationships in your life "rocking the boat"? Then call upon Him in prayer, and turn the pages of your Bible to see what He is speaking into your situation. He is still speaking to the wind and the waves.

During the times of turbulence in our lives, it is then that we must turn to Him for comfort and peace. "Be still, and know that

I am God …" (Psalm 46:10). As we are still in His Presence and quiet our troubled souls before Him, He makes Himself known to us and the peace that passes all understanding comes upon us.

In a way, it is easier to get into God's Presence during adversity because you don't like the place where you are (literally, mentally, or emotionally), so you want to get out of your current place or state of mind. I have found that when life is all good and there are little to no problems, I am content where I am, so I don't pursue His Presence like I should. Adversity then becomes a tool in the hand of the Lord used to work things together for our good by drawing us closer to Him. It is then that we run to Him with our cares of this world and draw upon the peace of His Presence to be ours.

Peace is a fruit of the Holy Spirit (see Galatians 5:22.) When we are filled with His Spirit, peace is grown in our hearts. That peace then becomes a part of our demeanor. Our peace then not only calms our hearts and minds, but overflows into others' lives as we come into contact with them. Rather than being blown over by the torrents of the world we live in, we become conduits of calm. Then we become "channels of His Peace" as prayerfully asked for in the old song, "Make me a channel of your Peace."

Prayer

Lord Jesus, my Prince of Peace, I call upon You to calm the storms of my heart and life. Arise in my soul and calm the waves of torrent. Speak into my heart and life divine strategies to defeat the storms that come at me. I cast my cares of this life upon You, and I thank you that you care for me so I don't have to. I turn my thoughts to You. I choose to meditate on You and Your Word. Come, Spirit of Peace, and dwell within my soul. Amen.

CHAPTER 4

Presents vs. Presence

Seek the LORD and His strength; seek His
face evermore!

~ PSALM 105:4 ~

WE ALL LOVE to receive presents. Christmas morning small
children eagerly await the moment they have been dreaming
of—the opening of their Christmas presents. The room is
filled with joyful expectation as they tear into the colorfully
wrapped gifts. Torn wrapping paper and bows fly through the
air as the hidden surprises are revealed. The air is filled with
joyful "oohhs" and "aahhs." Adults join the fun as they too
open their gifts. Age does not rob us of the joy of receiving a
gift. Even if we don't receive exactly what we want, the thought
behind the gift is important to us. And we always have the op-
tion of returning and exchanging it for something different.
Receiving presents is fun for people of all ages.

When I was a child, I can remember looking for my presents because I couldn't wait to see what it was that I was going

to receive. I would look under the bed, in the closets, in dresser drawers seeking for the hidden treasure—hoping to sneak a peek at what I would be soon receiving.

Our salvation is also a gift. Ephesians 2:8 tells us that our salvation is not anything we did, but is a gift from God—received by grace and through faith. People of faith are careful to point out to others and to teach their children that Christmas is not just about the giving and receiving of gifts but is about the greatest gift of all—the gift of Jesus Christ, God's only begotten Son, given to the world as a Savior to all who will receive Him. He is, as the saying goes, "The reason for the season"! We give and receive gifts on Christmas morning to celebrate the gift of Jesus Christ. John 3:16 tells us that "God so loved the world that He gave His only begotten Son, that whoever believes in Him should not perish but have everlasting life."

Just as a child's heart looks forward to receiving Christmas presents, so too we must have an expectant heart—a seeking heart, to seek out Jesus—our Christmas gift. The Bible tells us that unless we have childlike faith we will not receive His Kingdom (see Matt. 18:2-4; Mark 10:15; and Luke 18:17). We must seek for Him as a child seeks for their Christmas presents—with expectant and open hearts. I've heard it said that God loves to play hide and seek—He hides so we will seek Him. He is our Christmas gift. The gift of eternal life—Jesus—is given to all. But just as a present must be received by the participant, opened, and accepted, so too the gift of salvation must be received and accepted with an open heart. The best thing about the gift of Jesus is He is the perfect gift; there is no need to return Him for another, for He is the only one who qualifies to be the Savior of the world. He is the perfect gift for every open heart.

Sometimes when we open a present at Christmas, we feel that it is something we don't really need. In those cases we sometimes return the gift to the store because we are not in need of it. Therefore, to truly receive and appreciate a gift, we must realize that we are in need of it. Our salvation is like that too. If we don't realize that we are in need of it, we won't receive it. And I cannot emphasize enough it is not an "it" that we are in need of but a "Him". Our salvation is in the God-man Jesus Christ. We must realize how in need we are or we will never receive Him; He will remain an unwrapped gift to us.

The Need

The truth is, we are not an island unto ourselves. Rather, we are like men and women thrown overboard from a sinking ship with no one to save us. We cannot save ourselves for we cannot swim on our own strength forever. Jesus is our Life-Savior. Like a life guard springing to the rescue of a drowning victim, Jesus comes to our rescue to save us from sinking in an ocean of the world's currents sure to otherwise overwhelm us and take our lives. He left Heaven above to come to earth and be born a man-child so as to take our place and die in our place. For our lives, full of sin and destruction, would have soon destroyed us forever, but He traded places with us—each of us and drowned in the sea of sin for us as He hung on the cross. He then rose from the dead, conquering sin and death for us. Therefore, we, the otherwise drowning victims, can receive the gift of life—of salvation through our Life-Savior—Jesus Christ. Now, we can climb aboard a brand new ship—the ship of life in Christ Jesus. Now, we too are raised from the grave, alive in Him. No longer does the current of the world's pulls need to drag us under, no longer does the darkness of the world's deep problems need to overcome us, no longer do the waves of sin's wages need to rob us of the joy of life. Now we can climb aboard with Jesus and enjoy Him and the marvelous life He has to offer. He sails us to His various ports in life where we continue to renew our lives and receive the exports of Heaven. As we take His hand, He walks us out upon the water and causes us to overcome and rise above the otherwise destructive waters. Now, we have the power through Him to miraculously walk on the waters of life. By realizing our great need of Him, we cry out to Him and find Him. This is how we receive Him—the greatest gift.

The Gift that Keeps on Giving

Though Jesus is the greatest gift, He continues to bless us with His ongoing extravagant giving. The fourth chapter of Ephesians tells us that after His resurrection, Christ ascended back to Heaven and that he gave gifts to mankind. The gift of the five-fold ministry was given to us—Apostles, Prophets, Pastors, Evangelists, and Teachers who train and equip the rest of the body of Christ for the work of ministry. Each member of the body of Christ is also given gifts from Heaven to be used for the furthering of God's Kingdom. The Bible tells us to eagerly desire these gifts (see 1 Cor. 12:31; 1 Cor. 14:1). God desires to gift us so we can be co-laborers with Him in His Kingdom.

There is no end to God's giving. Every day we wake up is a blessing—a gift. Every breath we take is a gift. God gives us meaningful work and allows us to reap the fruit of our labors; this too is a gift from God. Though we work for our homes, cars, food, clothing and toys, they are actually gifts from God. Our relationships—husbands, wives, children, parents, siblings, peers—are all gifts from God. The freedom we have to worship Him openly in America is in fact a gift from God.

There is an old hymn called "Count your Many Blessings", and I have sung it many times as we led the nursing home ministry in our area. Though it is an old hymn, the truths do not age. We must count our blessings. Recognize the gifts God has given us and be thankful for them. Every good and perfect gift comes from God in Heaven. We are truly blessed.

Seeking His Face not His Hand

When You said, "Seek My face,"
my heart said to You, "Your face, LORD, I
will seek."

~ PSALM 27:8 ~

Prayer is the act of talking with our God who is always listening for our voice. The truth is ... we have a hotline to Heaven—prayer. His ear is always turned towards us to hear what it is we are saying to Him. The question is What do our prayers consist of? Are they simply a prayer list, or do they contain the ingredients of thanksgiving and praise? Are we praying simply to get answers or are we praying to spend time with our God, to be in His Presence and enjoy time with Him? Is our prayer life about presents or His Presence?

No one likes it when they only get a call from someone when they want something; you end up feeling "used." It is nice to get a call from someone who just wants to see how you are doing, and just wants to hear your voice. It is the same with God. While He wants to hear from us and desires to answer our petitions, He also just wants to spend time with His kids. He wants us to come to Him in humble prayer that desires for us to come into His Presence and just hang out for a while.

There are times when children desire to be held and loved on. When my oldest granddaughter was two years old, she would come to me while grabbing my legs and say, "Hold you, Hold you." She desired to be held close and loved. Likewise, as her grandmother there are times when I just desire to hold my granddaughters. No words even have to be spoken. I will hold her close and gently rock her in the rocking chair. During such times, we both feel loved and comforted. Likewise, there are times when we, as God's children, have a need to be comforted, held close, and loved on by our

Heavenly Father. During those times, we come to Him and say, "Just hold me close, Lord, hold me." He is so loving, kind, and gentle. He is the Father of all fathers. Even if our own fathers were absent, mean, nasty, or abusive, our Heavenly Father can heal us of all those bad memories and replace them with new memories based on experiences of being with Him and held in His gentle, yet strong arms. There are also times, however, when your Heavenly Father also desires to embrace you in His big, Father God arms and hold you close to Him. He also enjoys spending time with His kids. Spending time in His Presence—quiet time just enjoying Him—is a mutual time of peace and contentment.

However, often times what causes us to turn to God initially is our need. After coming to an end of our own ways, we discover that we cannot do life without Him. Many times it is after we have made a mess of things that we turn to God and ask Him to fix our problems. The great thing about God is He is always waiting for us to turn to Him and to return to Him. The truth is we need Him; we do! But when we return God doesn't just want to answer our prayers and fix our problems, He wants us to stay with Him—to be where He is and to be in relationship with Him.

God doesn't just want to bail us out of our troubles; no, He wants us to start doing life differently—dependent on Him for our every move. He wants to do life with us! Many times, however, we just want to get our needs met and then go on our merry ways. It is then that we are seeking merely His hand and not His face. God, however, doesn't want to give us a mere handout, He wants our life to be in His Presence. He wants to give us "face time."

When we want "face time" with someone it is about being in the same room with them; it is about a one-on one meeting. God's door is always open to us. He desires to have "face time" with us. As we look into our Heavenly Father's face, we behold His beauty, wisdom, and strength. His goodness shines upon us like the rays of the sun. "And His countenance was like the sun shining in its strength" (Revelation 1:16). We soak in His radiant love and are strengthened and at peace.

The Prodigal Son

We live in a world of broken families. Our earthly fathers are mere flesh and blood and sometimes fall short of what a good father should be. There are abusive fathers and absentee fathers. We have fathers who for sometimes selfish reasons, and sometimes reasons outside of their control, only send a support check and have no relationship with their children. The other side of the coin is we have older children who only want the money a father can give to support them and don't want to get to know their fathers. Either way, this is not what God desires for the family.

The Bible tells us a story of an older son, who doesn't initially desire a relationship with his father; he only wants what his father can give him. He sought his father's hand and not his face. Luke 15:11-21 tells us this story:

And he said, A certain man had two sons:

And the younger of them said to his father, Father, give me the portion of goods that falleth to me. And he divided unto them his living. And not many days after the younger son gathered all together, and took his journey into a far country, and there wasted his substance with riotous living. And when he had spent all, there arose a mighty famine in that land; and he began to be in want. And he went and joined himself to a citizen of that country; and he sent him into his fields to feed swine. And he would fain have filled his belly with the husks that the swine did eat: and no man gave unto him. And when he came to himself, he said, How many hired servants of my father's have bread enough and to spare, and I perish with hunger! I will arise and go to my father, and will say unto him, Father, I have sinned against heaven, and before thee, and am no more worthy to be called thy son: make me as one of thy hired servants. And he arose, and came to his father. But when he was yet a great way off, his father saw him, and had compassion, and ran, and fell on his neck, and kissed him. And the son said unto him, Father, I have sinned against heaven, and in thy sight, and am no more worthy to be called thy son (KJV).

This rebellious son had the nerve to ask for his inheritance before his father passed away. I cannot imagine doing such a thing! In essence, he was saying that he wished his father was dead! His father, however, out of love, gave his son his share of the inheritance. What love! This father no doubt was hurt by such a request, yet he did not show it. Rather he gave. "For God so loved the world, that he gave his only begotten Son, that whosoever believeth in him should not perish, but have everlasting life" (John 3:16 KJV).

The son then went on his own way, leaving his father behind. Clearly he was not interested in staying close by his father. He took the money and ran. His geographical distance was only a reflection of the relational distance between this father and son, for it seems there was no communication between them after his departure. As long as this young son had his natural needs met, he had no thoughts of home—no thoughts of his loving father.

After his money ran out, he had to find himself a job. Feeding pigs was the occupation that he found himself in. His new employment did not include meals or supply money for food for he thought of eating alongside of the pigs! The world has a way of using and abusing us. This son went out to enjoy the world, but ended up having no joy.

The day arrived when this young man "came to his senses." What a great day it is when it dawns on us that we have a Heavenly Father who cares for us. Though our earthly father may not care, or may not be present, yet our Heavenly Father waits for us! Though the world treats us bad, yet it can have a way of bringing us to our senses! This rebellious son remembered how well his father treated his hired servants in comparison to the employer he was under. This fact of life brought light into his otherwise dark heart. He realized that he had broken off relationship with his father and believed there was no way it could ever be the same. However, it dawned on him that he would return home not as a son but as a potential servant.

What a glorious day it is when we discover that we have been trying to do life alone, without the help and guidance of our Heavenly Father. What a great day it is when we come to our senses—when the light of God's Presence shines upon the dark areas of our life. We all have them—blind spots where we don't see clearly. These blind spots are actually places where we are deceived, and this deception causes us to make bad choices in life. But when the revelation of His love hits us—when the Way comes to reveal Himself and show us the "way" in life—we come to our senses, and His Presence leads us home—home to our Heavenly Father.

When this son returned home, however, his state was much different than when he left. He returned empty and humble. His stomach was no doubt empty, his pockets were no doubt empty, and his heart was also empty. The pride that once filled him was gone like his money. Sometimes it is when we lose it all that we discover we really had nothing. It is then that we have everything to gain. Not only was this young son's pocket book emptied of money, not only was his stomach emptied of food, but his heart was now emptied of pride, for he returned home *humble*. You see, when we return to our Father God after exhausting our own resourcefulness, what is in our heart and how we approach

Him matters, for "God resists the proud, But gives grace to the humble" (James 4:6).

This father, however, was watching for his son's return, and the Scriptures tell us that he saw him when he was yet a great way off. Our Heavenly Father is always watching us, even when we are a great way off. He watches us. He is watching and waiting ... always.

The joy this father exhibits in this story is but a bit of the joy that our Heavenly Father feels when we return home to Him. This father had compassion on his son and loved on him. Our Heavenly Father is tenderhearted and full of mercy and compassion. He will always meet us where we are when we are on our way home. When this son humbled himself and said he was not worthy to be called his son, that he only desired to be a servant, his father called for a robe and ring to be put on him, and he threw a party in his honor saying that his son was lost but now is found. He rejoiced in the return of His son. Likewise, when we come to our senses and come home to be with our Heavenly Father, there is great joy in all of Heaven. Though we don't deserve it, God welcomes us home and recognizes us as His sons and daughters! What a privilege, what an honor!

This son may have lost his monetary inheritance by squandering it away, yet he was blessed with a rich relationship with his father. Sometimes we have to suffer loss before we can realize our need. In losing, we gain. Like the prodigal son, we many times come to God to receive answers to prayers out of our need. We come looking for what lies in His hand. Yet,

our merciful and giving Father gives. He gives and then He
watches ... He watches for us to realize our true need—Him.

His Presence is Our Present

The truth is ... God's Presence is our present! There is no
greater present than to be in the Presence of God. He is the
ultimate gift. Salvation is the assurance of spending all of
eternity with Him—in His Presence. Faith is the practicing
of that reality—dwelling in His Presence—walking hand in
hand with our God.

In Old Testament times when the land of Canaan was being divided up into the portions of inheritance for the people
of Israel, the Levites—the priests—were not given a share of
that inheritance, and the reason was they had a better inheritance than mere property; *the Lord* was their inheritance (see
Deuteronomy 18:1-2)! Aaron, who was a priest, also was told that
he would have no inheritance in the land, and no portion among
the people, for the Lord was his portion and his inheritance.
The New Testament tells us that we are kings and *priests* (see
Revelation 1:6; 5:10). As His priest, God is our inheritance; He
is our portion forever and ever. Amen! Romans 8:17 tells us that
as children of God we are heirs of God and also joint-heirs with
Christ Jesus. Though He gives us all good things and has many
blessings to bestow upon us, yet He is the greatest blessing of all!
He is our all and all. Being in His Presence is our inheritance.

When we think of the word "inheritance," we tend to think
of someone dying in order to receive the blessing. For example,

when my parents passed away, my siblings and I received an inheritance from them. They put into writing in their last will and testimony what they desired each of us to receive. Likewise, God has written in His Word, the Bible, what He wills for each of us. We, like miners of a precious metal, mine out what is hidden inside for us. His Word is His will; it is written and so it is. The good news is we don't have to die before we can receive it! The writer of the will is the one, who has to die for the receiver to inherit it, and that person died over 2000 years ago; He is Jesus Christ our Lord. Not only did He die, but on the third day He rose again and is now seated at the right hand of our Father in Heaven. So now we can receive our inheritance. We don't have to wait until we die and go to Heaven to be with Him; we can be with Him now and always. He dwells with us by His Holy Spirit.

Wrapped Up in Him

Having received Him—our gift of salvation, we have received the greatest gift of all time; nothing can compare. Having received Him, we learn to come into His Presence on a daily basis, and our lives become more and more "wrapped up in Him." For us this means that we become more and more focused on Him and conscious of His Presence. But the amazing thing is when our lives become "wrapped up" in Him, like a gift on Christmas morning all wrapped up and tied with a bow, we also become a gift to the Lord! He too is very joyful and happy to receive our hearts as His place to dwell. A heart that is given to Him is His greatest gift! When we are wrapped up in Him, we are His gift as well.

Prayer

Lord Jesus, You are the greatest gift. Forgive me for times when I have only come into Your Presence to receive something from Your hand. I recognize now afresh how precious a gift Your Presence is. You are the greatest gift. You are my inheritance and my portion. You are my present.You are all I truly need. Abide with me now I pray. Amen.

CHAPTER 5

§

Abiding in His Presence

And I will dwell in the house of the LORD
forever.

~ PSALM 23:6 ~

WHEN I RECALL my childhood, I remember going to my good
friend's house to play. We would laugh and play all day long—
indoors, outdoors—never running out of things to do. Finally
the dreaded time arrived—the time to go home. I didn't want
to go home because I was so enjoying being with my friend.
I wanted to stay with her and play longer. So, my friend and I
would beg and plead with our moms, "Pleeeese … can't I stay
longer, pleeeese?" The two moms would discuss it and usually
they would end up extending my stay.

Best friends are the best! You can confide in them and
dream with them. Friends share their hopes and dreams with
each other. Friends want to stay in each other's company. Jesus
said, "No longer do I call you servants, for a servant does not
know what his master is doing; but I have called you friends, for
all things that I heard from My Father I have made known to

you ..." (John 15:15). Just like when we get closer to an acquaintance and they then become our "friend," Jesus also upgrades our status: He considers us not just servants, but "friends." He desires to draw us close to Him. He wants us to stay with Him, just like a dear friend stays over at your house to be with you. He too wants to come to "stay." A close friend longs to be with you, and you in turn long to be with your close friend. Jesus calls us friends; that means He longs to be with us. Just like we ask to stay longer at a friend's house, so also, we can ask for His Presence to linger. He desires us to have that same "childlike faith." We call upon Him to stay with us, and to make His Presence known in our lives. "Be with me, Lord, and stay with me Lord, in a tangible way please" can be a prayer that we offer up to Him on a continual basis (both verbally and silently in our hearts.) *It is no accident that the Lord put this verse about being called a "friend" of God (John 15:15) in the chapter about "abiding in the vine" because cultivating that deep friendship with Jesus is a secret to "abiding in His Presence."*

To have our friend come over to our house, we typically invite them. We want our friend to feel welcome, so we ask them to come over and spend some time with us, or to accompany us on a trip or outing. It is no different with the Lord. We must ask Him to come to our house. The Holy Spirit is a gentleman, and He desires an invitation. He wants to be wanted. He desires for you to desire Him. When you invite Him, He will come. The wonderful thing about the Lord is His calendar is never too full to find time for you. Unlike us, God is omnipresent. That means that God can be many places at once. I wish I could be in more than one place at a time, but that is not possible; that is a trait that is God's alone.

God's itinerary is not full on His end; no, it is our schedules that get filled up. We have so many things that pull at our time: family, work, volunteer work, recreation, commitments, and even God's work can take away our time from just spending it with Him. Our lives get so busy. We have to make sure to make room for God in our busy schedules. Sunday mornings are just not enough. We need to meet with God every day. Taking special time in His Word and in prayer is essential to keeping this friendship with God a real and abiding relationship. Just like not seeing a friend or talking with them puts distance between you and them, so also when we don't talk with God and take time to hear His Word puts distance between us and Him relationally. He is a relational God and He desires to be present with us.

Moment by Moment

Relationship with God is a bit like a marriage. He calls us up, like a gentleman calls a woman and asks her out on a date. God too calls upon us. We are drawn to Him much like an attraction between a man and woman. We feel spiritually drawn to Him. As we walk with Him, we get to know Him just like in a relationship of two friends. We share our hearts with Him, and He in turn shares His heart with us. That is why he said in John 15:15 that we are no longer servants but friends, because a servant doesn't know what the Master is doing; in other words, there is no sharing of the Master's heart or personal business. But friends share their hearts with each other. Jesus said that all things He has heard from His Father He shares with us. He holds back nothing. Now that is a true friend! He trusts us with His secrets.

Even as a man asks the love of his life to be his forever in marriage, so too Jesus asks us to be His bride and to be forever His (see 2 Corinthians 11:2-3; Revelation 19:7-9). The giving of our lives to Him is our salvation. It is then that we become His bride—forever His, only death will not do us part! What a wonderful union, our souls knit together with His. This is a blessed union and holy matrimony.

When with our spouse, we enjoy both intimate moments and less intimate moments. We go places together and work together. We also have fun together and have times of just "hanging out." It is no different with the Holy Spirit of God. We are to have those special times with Him, but it should not end there. *The secret to abiding in Him is to be ever mindful of His Presence, moment by moment.* His Presence must be cultivated on a moment by moment basis. This is how we abide in Him. By being mindful of His Presence, we adore Him, we talk with Him, and He with us. Sometimes His Presence just comes upon us and we are embraced with His peace and joy. When trouble strikes, He strengthens us and comforts us. He is an ever-present help in times of trouble, because he is *ever present.* He is always there to help us in troubled times (see Psalm 46:1.) We need only to acknowledge His Presence, and He will make Himself known to us.

When my husband is in the other room, I yell out, "Mike, Mike! Are you here?" He then answers me, "Yes, I am here." It is no different with Jesus. When you don't sense His Presence, all you need to do is call out to Him, "Jesus, Jesus! Are you here?" He will then make His Presence known to you and reassure you that He is with you. Jesus said, "I will never leave you and never forsake you" (Hebrews 13:5). His Holy Spirit comforts us as we call upon Him. We are never alone.

We Are Never Alone

Nevertheless I am continually with You; You
hold me by my right hand.

~ Psalms 73:23 ~

Loneliness is a big problem in some people's lives. People need relationships. God said it is not good for man to be alone and, therefore, He made not just Adam but Eve as well (see Genesis 2:18). While it is true that we all have times when we want "alone time" without the intrusion of other people, yet we need each other; we need fellowship—companionship of some kind. People search for relationship online, on social media, dating networks, and even at church. While there is a time and place for all this, *God* wants to fill those voids in our lives *first* and *foremost*. Sometimes He will keep us from finding that "special someone" until we can learn to put Him first. He desires to be our "special someone." He is the ultimate mate, friend, brother, and lover of our soul. God will fill every need and empty hole in our souls, if we let Him. He is just waiting to be asked, longing to be longed for, and desiring to be desired! He is our "knight in shining armor" and He is waiting for us to notice that He is right there, *waiting*. His Word says, "*Let your* conduct *be* without covetousness; *be* content with such things as you have. For He Himself has said, 'I will never leave you nor forsake you'" (Hebrews 13:5). It is interesting that He first tells us to be content with what we have and not to covet, then He follows it with the fact that He is always there. That is because His Presence is to be enough. We are to look to Him, and He will provide all we need. He is all we need! He is forever faithful to His Word. God is smiling upon you. He is watching you and caring for you. He feels your pain, and wants to make all things new in your life. You need only to turn your eyes upon Jesus, and allow Him to look into your soul and minister to your needs. Your faith has eyes to see Him, your faith has ears to hear Him, and your faith has senses to sense Him.

When His Spirit shows up in a "tangible way", He gives the best "goose bumps" I have ever felt. He replaces those fleshy feelings we have with *godly grace*. God has a way of transforming our day and transforming our lives as we look to Him and His Word.

I Won't Let Go!

I remember as a small child taking hold of my mother's leg and not wanting to let go as I looked up at her. I wanted her to hold me, and I didn't want to let go of her. She used to say things like, "I have to get my work done; let go of me." But I would laugh and say, "Nope, I am never letting go!" So too, should be our heart towards God our Savior. Take hold of Him and never let go!

Jacob in the Old Testament was one who had a similar gripping encounter with the Lord. Before crossing over into his land of promise, Jacob, who had been at odds with his brother Esau as a result of his own striving and deceptive dealings, sought to be at peace with his brother. He sent his wife and children ahead of him and was then left alone. We all need alone time to seek God and meet with Him. Though we meet with Him on the Sabbath corporately—with the body of believers—we also need to get away from our brothers, sisters, and family for some intense alone time with God. After sending his family ahead of him Jacob found himself alone with God. It is then that he entered into a manifestation of the Lord's Presence (see Genesis 32:24, 30; Isaiah 63:9; and Hosea 12:4). Jacob wrestled with the Lord in what seems like an actual wrestling match. We also wrestle with God in times of prayer as we cry out for our deliverance from the taunts of life and for the deliverance of our loved ones.

We see in Genesis 32:26 as this encounter continued, the Lord's Presence said, "Let Me go, for the day breaks." But Jacob answered, "I will not let You go unless you bless me!" Though we receive many blessings from the Lord, the greatest blessing of all is HIM. Having His Presence with us and touching our lives is in fact the greatest blessing. And, like Jacob, our hearts should cry with, "I'll not let you go, ever!" When in His Presence, ask Him to stay. Tell Him that you never want to let Him go! When His Presence starts to lift, cry out with, "Don't go. I want You. I need You!" His Presence is our blessing. Asking for His Presence to stay is a secret of abiding in His Presence.

Abiding in the Vine

> Abide in Me, and I in you. As the branch
> cannot bear fruit of itself, unless it abides in
> the vine, neither can you,
> unless you abide in Me.
>
> ~ JOHN 15:4 ~

Jesus tells us that we must abide or stay connected to Him in the same way that a branch stays connected to the vine. He is our vine—our life-flow. If we cut ourselves off from Him, we will wither and dry-up spiritually. There needs to be a life-flow coming from His Spirit into ours all day long. It is by His Spirit that we receive Words of life from Him. He imparts grace to us by His Spirit. We must stay connected. Like an electric appliance must stay plugged into the electrical socket, so too, we must stay plugged into Him. We are connected Spirit to spirit. We stay connected in our thoughts. Think on Him. Think on His Word. When we give Him our attention and thoughts, we are worshipping Him in our hearts. "... 'You shall love the LORD your God with all your heart, with all

your soul, with all your strength, and with all your mind..."
(Luke 10:27). So throughout our day we think on Him, and
thank Him for all He has done. We pray for those that come to
mind, and we are aware of His Presence. What a lovely place
to be.

If we don't stay connected to Him, we lose our fruitfulness. Just like if you were to cut a branch off from an apple
tree, it would be incapable of producing apples, so too we are
incapable of producing fruit for God if we are not staying
connected to Him in relationship. We must abide in Him—
the Vine. When we are connected to Him in relationship
we receive a flow of grace from His Spirit that brings life
to our souls. Let your heart reach out to Him even now.
"Come Holy Spirit, come and flow in our hearts and lives."
He is there with His grace bringing strength into your soul.
*Everything you need to be nurtured and grow is present in His
Presence.*

When we lack in fruitfulness, we need to call out to Him
and return to Him with sincerity of heart. Usually, I find that
if I haven't been with Him as I should, there is a tinge of guilt
within me—my own heart condemns me. The remedy for this
is really simple: simply pray a quick prayer asking God to forgive you for not talking to Him lately and whatever else the
Holy Spirit is convicting you of. God will forgive you. This
prayer of faith will wash your conscience and allow you to get
plugged back in with Him. The enemy of your soul wants to
condemn you. Condemnation is intended by the enemy to
make you feel unworthy. When we feel unworthy, we avoid

God. When we avoid God, we stay under condemnation and sink into despair. When we sink into despair, we want to go eat worms. Don't go eat worms … call upon Him and be restored!

Being restored in relationship with Him is simple but it requires us to make a quality decision to do so and to change our habits. We must be "ever-mindful" of Him. Keep God in your thoughts throughout the day. Talk to Him often; by doing so, you are praying without ceasing. "Rejoice always, pray without ceasing, in everything give thanks; for this is the will of God in Christ Jesus for you" (1 Thessalonians 5:16-18). I have found that when I am ever-mindful of Him, not only do I remember to pray about the troubles and challenges of the day, but I also find that I am more thankful for what blessings the day has in store. We can't be in His Presence and commune with Him long without having a heart full of thanksgiving. That is because we are reminded of all that He has done for us. Even if He never did another thing for me, I am forever thankful for the salvation He has won for me and given me so freely. I am forever thankful for all He did to suffer and die in my place.

Abiding In His Word

We cannot abide in Christ if we are not abiding in His Word. As we give ourselves to His Word, His Spirit meets with us and makes it personal to us. He speaks through His Word. Christ and His Word are one: "In the beginning was the Word, and the Word was with God, and the Word was God" (John 1:1). "And the Word became flesh and dwelt among us, and we beheld His glory, the glory as of the only begotten of the Father, full of grace and truth" (John 1:14). Jesus and His Word are inseparable. Because Christ Jesus speaks to us through His Word, we say the Word is *alive*.

When we daily read His Word, He feeds us and gives us strength, for we do not live by mere bread alone but by every Word that proceeds from God's mouth (see Matthew 4:4). We need His Word to feed our spirit-man and keep us spiritually fit. We are a spirit, we live in a body, and we possess a soul (which is comprised of our mind, will, and emotions). If we don't feed our Spirit the Word of God on a daily basis, we will become spiritually weak and have no strength to live a victorious life in Christ. Jesus said to pray, "Give us this day our daily bread" (Matthew 6:11), this is not just physical food, but spiritual food as well. We are in fact saying, "Feed me Lord Your Word for I need You and Your sustenance daily."

The Word of God washes us and makes us clean, that is why Jesus said, "You are already clean because of the word which I have spoken to you" (John 15:3). His Word washes over us, and as we apply it to our lives, we are made clean. Ephesians 5:26 says that we are cleansed by the "washing of water by the word." We are forgiven and our sins are washed away by His blood and by faith in Him, but we are made holy and kept clean by applying His Word to our daily lives.

When we spend time with Him in His written Word, we are storing up His wisdom within ourselves. The saying goes, "You are what you eat." Well, spiritually speaking, this is also true. What we put in our spirits is what comes out. Jesus said, " But the

Helper, the Holy Spirit, whom the Father will send in My name, He will teach you all things, and bring to your remembrance all things that I said to you" (John 14:26). His Holy Spirit brings His Word to our memories and "highlights" it for us. He teaches us how to apply it to our lives and walk it out; therefore, it is impossible to abide in Him without abiding in His Word also. When God speaks to us, while it is sometimes a quote from the Scriptures, other times, it is not. However, everything we hear in the spirit needs to be tested by comparing it to the whole of God's Word. The Scripture tells us to "Test all things; hold fast what is good" (see 1Thessalonians 5:21-22). It is by searching and knowing the Scriptures that we are able to test all the things we hear. If it agrees with God's written Word, hold onto it; if it conflicts, throw it out! "All Scripture *is* given by inspiration of God, and *is* profitable for doctrine, for reproof, for correction, for instruction in righteousness" (2 Timothy 3:16).

A Great Blessing for Abiding

If you abide in Me, and My words abide in
you, you will ask what you desire, and it shall
be done for you.

~ JOHN 15:7 ~

As if the blessing of His Presence is not enough, He offers us yet another blessing for abiding with Him: Our Lord says that if we will abide with Him and in His Word, then He will give us the desires of our hearts (see Psalm 37:4; John 15:7). This is like receiving a signed blank check. And this is why when we abide in Him and in His Word, His will and His Word then abides in us. We dwell with Him and His will, Word, and ways are slowly made known to us as we seek Him. He reveals His thoughts to us, and we conform to them. Therefore, we only want what He wants. Our desires are changed into what He desires. When this happens, our prayers change. We no longer pray selfish prayers that will get unanswered, but we ask for His will to be done in our lives. "You ask and do not receive, because you ask amiss, that you may spend it on your pleasures" (James 4:3). However, when we pray according to His Word and will, He answers: "Now this is the confidence that we have in Him, that if we ask anything according to His will, He hears us" (1 John 5:14). God's Word reveals His will, however, when we are not sure how to pray, we can always pray as Jesus did in the garden, "Father, if it is Your will, take this cup away from Me; nevertheless not My will, but Yours, be done" (Luke 22:42). Then we need to let Him answer the prayer *His way* and *in His timing.*

What a joy to know that as we become one with Him, our will conforms to His and therefore our prayers are according to His Word and will. Abiding with Him is all about becoming one with Him. The vine and the branches are one; they only become separate when the branches are broken off from the vine. When we abide with Him, we are "attached." Did you ever get "attached" to someone? There can be good attachments and bad attachments, but being attached to God is the best attachment of them all!

Some people want to be attached to Jesus but don't want to spend time in His Word. God and His Word are one. We cannot abide in Christ without abiding in His Word; they go hand in hand. His blessing of answered prayer can only be found as we abide both in Him and in His Word. "Delight yourself also in the LORD, and He shall give you the desires of your heart (Psalm 37:4). His Presence is a delight to our soul. "I will delight myself in Your statutes; I will not forget Your word. Your testimonies also are my delight and my counselors" (Psalm 119:16, 24). His Presence is found in His Word.

Practicing His Presence

I remember years ago when the Lord was teaching me how to abide in His Presence, He used a little book to help to teach me: *Practicing the Presence of God* by Brother Lawrence. Brother Lawrence was born in France in 1614 and because he was poor, he chose to join the army. He later had an experience with the Lord Jesus Christ. His life was reborn and forever changed. As a result, he joined the Carmelite Monastery. At the monastery he was given the mundane task of working in the kitchen and cleaning pots and pans. As he diligently worked, he learned how to "practice the Presence of the Lord." He practiced abiding in Christ as he labored over a sink full of dishes!

The spirit and character of the man so attracted others that they would ask him what the secret of his relationship with Christ was; this led Brother Lawrence to begin to share his practice with others. He began to write down his practice of God's Presence in little writings that he called "maxims." After his death, those in the church that admired Brother Lawrence and learned from him compiled his writings into a book. Today Brother Lawrence's writings are a blessing to both Catholics and Protestants alike who are longing for a deeper and more intimate relationship with Christ our Lord.

The Lord led me to this book by speaking directly to me to "Practice His Presence" and then while I was in an antique shop, He spoke it to me again and then led me to the book that was eagerly awaiting me on the dusty bookshelf. I now am proud to own one of the early copies of the book; its pages are yellowed and brittle, but its truths and meanings are fresh and inspiring. Brother Lawrence's book is a classic and can be purchased at nearly any place where Christian books are sold.

Brother Lawrence taught that the most mundane task could be turned into a method of abiding in the love of Christ. He found that it was not important what task one was doing, but what was important was the motive behind doing it. During the time I first was led to His book, I was then working at my father's grocery store. One of my "mundane tasks" was to take care of the returned bottles and cans. This was a job that every one of our employees dreaded for the returns were often times filthy; sometimes they had bugs in them, and occasionally they were used as a spittoon and therefore filled with sticky smelly chewing tobacco! Yuck! Being inspired by Brother Lawrence's book, I began to change the way I viewed this humdrum and dirty job. Instead of seeing it as the dreaded chore, I now saw it as a divine opportunity to get alone with the Lord and practice His Presence. It provided an escape from my working with the public where I could steal a few precious moments with the lover of my soul. Like lovers who hide away to steal a kiss, I would long to find Him there where our spirits met. "Kiss the Son, lest He be angry ..." (Psalm 2:12). He is a jealous God and His Spirit longs for you. I found Him there while alone in the bottle room. The tangibility of His Spirit awaited me as my soul longed and anticipated His Presence. It was during this time that I learned what it meant to do all things as unto the Lord. "And whatever you do, do it heartily, as to the Lord and not to men, knowing that from the Lord you will receive the reward of the inheritance; for you serve the Lord Christ" (Colossians 3:23-24). I found that as I did this as "unto the Lord" and invited His Presence, He showed up and did the job with me just like a friend gives you a helping hand. At times His Presence would be so strong that I could barely finish the task, for His Presence would overwhelm me. This is the delight of His Presence we can all experience in our everyday lives. No matter what mundane task awaits our day: washing pots and pans, sorting dirty bottles and cans, or any other job (great or small) can all be transformed into an altar from which to worship Him. This is abiding in Christ.

Prayer

Jesus, lover of my soul, be with me every moment of my day. I give you my day today and every day. Meet with me in the morning and be my companion throughout my day. Speak to me through your Word, for You and Your Word are one. Manifest Your Presence to me now I pray and be ever so close to me. I love you so much. Don't ever leave me, Lord. Remind me to embrace Your Presence and to do all things as unto You. I long for You to be with me—now and always. Amen.

CHAPTER 6

—— § ——

The Fruitfulness of His Presence

I am the vine, you are the branches. He who
abides in Me, and I in him, bears much fruit;
for without Me you can do nothing.

~ JOHN 15:5 ~

To ABIDE IN Christ is to remain connected to Him. Some versions of the Bible actually use the word *remain* in place of *abide*. He is the vine and we are the branches. Without Him, like a branch that is separated from the vine, we will wither and die spiritually. A branch that is separated from Him cannot bear fruit; it cannot even keep itself alive but will shrivel up and die because there is no life flowing through it. Without Him we can do nothing. He is our life. Our very next breath is only possible because of Him. As we realize this fact *and dwell in that reality*, our lives becomes filled with thanksgiving for the life He gives, and this gives our lives meaning; we are then filled with the life that flows forth from Him—the Vine.

This flowing forth of spiritual life from the Spirit of God is what produces the fruit of the Spirit in our life. Because He is in our life, His fruit is grown. This fruit is supernatural in our lives; yet, when we stay connected to Him, it grows naturally in our lives. The fruit of the Holy Spirit is listed in Galatians 5:22-23: love, joy, peace, longsuffering, kindness, goodness, faithfulness, gentleness, and self-control. This fruit is what produces godly character in our lives and is only obtained from staying connected to the Vine—the Lord Jesus Christ.

Love — The love of God is described in 1 Corinthians 13. The gifts of the Spirit operate through love. "Though I speak with the tongues of men and of angels, but have not love, I have become sounding brass or a clanging cymbal. And though I have the gift of prophecy, and understand all mysteries and all knowledge, and though I have all faith, so that I could remove mountains, but have not love, I am nothing" (1 Corinthians 13:1-2). God's love here is the word *agape* in the Greek. Agape love is unlike mere human love for it is God's love. It is the kind of love that is selfless and sacrificial. Jesus came to earth to save us because of the love of God. "For God so loved the world that He gave His only begotten Son, that whoever believes in Him should not perish but have everlasting life" (John 3:16). The love of God is giving, it helps others, and it is kind. Christ Jesus endured the beatings, scourging, mocking, pain, suffering, and humiliation all for you and for me because He loves us so much. This love flows forth from Him to you and for you. As we stay connected to Him, we sip the goodness of Him and fill our tanks with this love, for you see—He lavishes that love upon us so that we can feel it and be filled with it and have it to give to others. God's love is unique and different than the love of the world. It is not selfish. This agape love of God is greater than the mere love of the human heart. If we do not stay connected to Him, we run out of this love to give, for we can only get our supply from Him. There is no other source. We cannot generate it on our own. There is no "home-brew", there is no "still" we can set up in our back-woods to stir up a batch of agape love. No, it is only found and received by staying connected to the source—Jesus Christ. As we stay connected to Him—the Vine—we receive this agape love into our very being. It is a life-flow that produces the Spirit-filled life we live. When we are filled with His Spirit, we are filled with love, for God is love (see 1 John 4:8). When we call upon His Presence we tap into His love flow. "Now hope does not disappoint, because the love of God has been poured out in our hearts by the Holy Spirit who was given to us" (Romans 5:5). This is done by faith and yielding to Him.

Love is like God in liquid form for God's Spirit flows into our lives through His love. This love feeds us and then flows from us in order to help others. If we don't receive God's love into our lives, we in turn will not have any to give to others. God's love meets our inmost needs. Apostle Paul said that nothing can separate us from God's love: "For I am persuaded that neither death nor life, nor angels nor principalities nor powers, nor things present nor things to come, nor height nor depth, nor any other created thing, shall be able to separate us from the love of God which is in Christ Jesus our Lord" (Romans 8:38-39).

The love of God glues us together in relationships. We need His love flowing into our lives and from our lives or we will inevitably become isolated and alone. It is His love that keeps us connected to people. He holds all things together (see Colossians 1:17). Apostle Paul exhorts the church to speak the truth in love and to grow together under the leadership of Jesus Christ. "From whom the whole body, joined and knit together by what every joint supplies, according to the effective working by which every part does its share, causes growth of the body for the edifying of itself in love" (Ephesians 4:16). His love is the bond that holds our families and body of believers together. May we all grow in the rich soil of God's love and stay connected.

Joy — This fruit is given to us by God for our pleasure and delight. It is a state of being that causes us to be overwhelmed with the pleasure of God's Presence. "For You have made him most blessed forever; You have made him exceedingly glad with Your presence" (Psalm 21:6). When we dwell in His Presence, He is delighted and we feel his delight; we in turn are delighted with the joy of His Presence. This joy of the soul is deeper than any temporary worldly pleasure. The joy of the Lord is not based on the material things of this world. This joy gives us strength to carry on through any trouble the world throws at us. When we dwell in the joy of His Presence, we will be able to stand under the pressures of the day, "for the joy of the LORD is your strength" (Nehemiah 8:10). When we let go of His Presence, we let go of our joy; when we let go of our joy, we let go of our strength! But we are strengthened when we call upon His Presence. He comes by His Spirit and strengthens us and our joy returns—the joy of our salvation— the joy of His Presence! The Psalmist wrote of this joy when he said, "In Your presence is fullness of joy; at Your right hand are pleasures forevermore" (Psalm 16:11). Nothing the world has to offer can be compared to the pleasure of being in His Presence! This joy of the Lord that is our delight, that is our pleasure, that is our strength, can abide with us as we abide in Him; it does not have to fade like the happiness the world has to offer. Jesus said after speaking about abiding in Him, "These things I have spoken to you, that My joy may remain in you, and that your joy may be full" (John 15:11). He wants us to be full of His joy and for it to remain with us!

Joy can launch us into joyful dance! David's dance unto the Lord was no doubt an expression of joy (see 2 Samuel 6:14-23). It is by coming into His Presence that we find true joy. Coming into His Presence gives us reason to rejoice. "For in Him we live and move and have our being ..." (Acts 17:28). Even the unborn John the Baptist leaped for joy while still in his mother's womb when in the Presence of Jesus who also was yet unborn and residing in His mother Mary's womb! (See Luke 1:39-41.) And Jesus Himself, during His earthly ministry, rejoiced greatly when He saw His disciples operating in His power and directives (see Luke 10:18-21). Living and moving in His Presence brings mutual joy to Him and us!

There are times, however, when being joyful is a sacrifice that we offer up to God. This is because we get focused on our cares of life. This can bring us down and drain us of our joy in Him. However, when we remember that joy is found in Him, we then can refocus and offer Him up a joyful sacrifice.

> And now my head shall be lifted up above my
> enemies all around me;
> therefore I will offer sacrifices of joy in His
> tabernacle;
> I will sing, yes, I will sing praises to the
> LORD.

~ PSALM 27:6 ~

When we focus on all He has done for us and all that His Word says about us, we have reason to rejoice. He also turns our mourning into dancing (see Psalms 30:11).

It is no accident that God created His people and placed them in a garden called Eden where His Presence dwelt and His people walked and talked with Him, for the word Eden means *delight*, and there is indeed delight for our souls in His wonderful Presence. Return to the place of "delight"—it is there with Him that we were intended to dwell. It is there that He transforms our wilderness into the fruit of Eden.

For the LORD will comfort Zion,
He will comfort all her waste places;
He will make her wilderness like Eden,
and her desert like the garden of the LORD;
joy and gladness will be found in it,
thanksgiving and the voice of melody.

~ Isaiah 51:3 ~

Peace — We all want peace. The truth is in the world we are going to have trouble, but God's Spirit is longing to flow through our very hearts and to keep our souls in peace. He is the Prince of Peace who leads us and even carries us through the troubles of this life. His peace is stronger than our fears and troubles. It has a staying power that holds us if we yield to it. His peace keeps us from being overwhelmed with anxiety and worry. Though we may not have the answers to all our problems yet His peace resides within because we yield to Jesus, the Prince of Peace. "You will keep him in perfect peace, whose mind is stayed on You, because he trusts in You" (Isaiah 26:3). Turning our thoughts to Him and letting go of our struggles in His Presence fills our hearts with the peace that can only come from Him. As we give Him our cares and troubles, He gives us His peace in exchange.

Fear, anxiety, and depression can sometimes take over in our hearts and lives. But Jesus came to free us from these bondages. He came to set the captives free (see Luke 4:18). As we call upon Him, He delivers us from these foes. "And let the peace of God rule in your hearts, to which also you were called in one body; and be thankful (Colossians 3:15). The key word in this Scripture is "let." The Amplified Bible describes the peace of God ruling in our hearts to that of an umpire. When you think about how an umpire rules in a ball game, he calls the shots. He will declare what is "safe" and what is "out." That is what we must do. When thoughts come up that are fear-based, they are not "safe" thoughts; therefore, call them "out!" Then replace them with godly "safe" thoughts that bring life and comfort and are based on His Word.

Being in right relationship with God brings peace to our souls. When He is Lord all is well with our souls. When Jesus is not just Savior of our lives but truly *Lord*, it is then that the Prince of Peace is ruling upon the throne of our hearts. This topic of peace is so sought after that I devoted an entire chapter to it: "The Peace of His Presence." Come into His Presence, my friend, and find peace and rest for your soul.

Longsuffering — Some Bible versions translate the word long-suffering as patience. Having patience is something we many times don't want to do, yet it is a virtue of Christ that we are to practice. The New International Version of the Bible translates longsuffering as forbearance. This fruit causes us to be able to bear with people. We then are strong in the Lord with the strength and fortitude that come from His Presence. This fruit keeps us from giving up and quitting when we are feeling frustrated. This fruit can be plentiful in our lives as we abide in Him—The Vine.

The Lord Himself, when He manifested Himself to Moses before giving Him the second set of Ten Commandments, introduced Himself by proclaiming His Name before Moses by describing His virtues: "And the LORD passed before him and proclaimed, 'The LORD, the LORD God, merciful and gracious, *longsuffering*, and abounding in goodness and truth, keeping mercy for thousands, forgiving iniquity and transgression and sin, by no means clearing the guilty, visiting the iniquity of the fathers upon the children and the children's children to the third and the fourth generation'" (Exodus 34:6-7, emphasis mine). It is no accident that the Lord revealed Himself to Moses in this way *after* Moses broke the first set of the stone Commandments in his total frustration of the people when he saw their acts of idolatry that occurred while he was on the mountain top in God's Presence. God revealed His mercy, graciousness, and longsuffering to Moses. He was revealing to Moses that He possessed these qualities and Moses also needed to practice these qualities in his life and ministry as well. After Moses received this humbling revelation, he interceded for the people (himself included) that God would forgive them all, though they had been a "stiffed necked people," and that they would become God's inheritance (see Exodus 32:9-14). Likewise, when we are reminded of how longsuffering God is with us, it causes us to pray for others and to have longsuffering patient endurance for them. Later, Moses was able to remind God of His own Word describing Himself as "longsuffering" when God was ready to cut off His people after they rejected Him over and over again by testing Him with doubt and unbelief. In Moses' prayer He reminded the Lord of what He said about who He was, and God in turn forgave the Israelites (see Numbers 14:11-19). However, their sin of disobedience caused them to miss out on the opportunity to come into their Promise Land. Even though we can be forgiven of our sins, yet we also can reap sins' painful consequences in our lives. The Lord is patient and bears with us with His longsuffering; therefore, we also are to have these attributes in our lives and ministries (see 2 Corinthians 6:4-7).

Apostle Paul prayed that the Colossians would walk in a manner that pleased the Lord and would be strengthened by the Lord's mighty power to bear the fruit of patience and longsuffering along with joy and thanksgiving to God (see Colossians 1:10-11). Apostle Paul also speaks of longsuffering as part of the Christian's clothing to be worn daily (see Colossians 3:12). In 1 Timothy 1:16, Apostle Paul also tells us that he received mercy that the longsuffering from the Lord Jesus Christ would be manifested in his life in order that he might become a pattern for others to follow (see 1 Timothy 1:16). We also, like Paul, can receive the Lord's merciful longsuffering and then show it forth to others. As we surrender and yield to the Lord Jesus Christ, we receive and reveal this sweet fruit to others around us who then, in turn, may taste and see that the Lord is good, as we point the way to Him. His fruit is most desirable!

I've heard it said not to pray for patience because then God will give you those undesirable opportunities to have to practice it. However, opportunities to run out of patience are quite plentiful in life regardless. We must call upon Him in prayer to help give us the strength to endure under the pressures of life. It is only by calling on Him for strength that we can receive and show forth this fruit of longsuffering. Then He pours forth His strength in our lives by His Spirit and we find ourselves flowing in His grace.

"The Lord is not slack concerning His promise, as some count slackness, but is longsuffering toward us, not willing that any should perish but that all should come to repentance" (2 Peter 3:9). The Lord has great patience with each and every one of us; He bears with us and is merciful. Reminding ourselves of His patient longsuffering with us brings a great gratitude in our hearts and causes us to want to be like Him by extending this virtue to others.

Patient longsuffering is to be a part of our lives. As we abide in His Presence we will receive a never ending supply of this fruit that will give us endurance to finish well. We then will have the strength to never, ever give up, and will be able to echo Apostle Paul's words, "I have fought the good fight, I have finished the race, I have kept the faith" (2 Timothy 4:7).

Kindness – Kind acts are shown by us as an expression of a loving, kind heart. Jesus Christ Himself demonstrated the ultimate act of kindness by coming to the world and suffering and dying for us (see Ephesians 2:7). We now, through His example and by His power, can demonstrate true kindness to those we encounter daily. Because of His ultimate act of kindness, we too can live an abundant life of grace and be fruitful in Him. Because He lives we also live and abide in Him. Our abiding in the Vine allows us to reach out with expressions of kindness to others as we are inspired by His Holy Spirit to do so. Our hands become His in reaching out to others in acts of kindness that speak of His love and compassion. When we abide in Him, our kindness is an expression of His. And we have an opportunity to point to Him when others thank us for our acts of kindness.

Kindness is also translated "gentleness" in the King James Version of the Bible. Our acts of kindness are done through a spirit of gentleness. Kind acts of gentleness are a response of the Holy Spirit within us. Our natural inclination of striking back when injured can be transformed into a loving and gentle response of kindness by the Holy Spirit within us. By abiding in Him moment by moment, His Spirit reminds us to react differently than the world would (we are in the world but not of it). As we draw grace from Him—the Vine, we are able to receive the strength of gentleness to turn the other cheek when attacked and persecuted (see Luke 6:29). This can only be done through Him because it is not a natural response, but a supernatural response. This response of loving-kindness can have a shocking effect on the receiver because it is not natural. Gentle kindness is love in action. Luke 6:35-36 tells us to love our enemies and explains how God is kind to the unthankful and the evil. We, too, must react to unthankful and mean people with His kindness. This fruit of kindness is expressed by the power of the Spirit to impact the unbeliever and wake them up to the love of God. His loving-kindness is shocking to them especially when we are turning the other cheek, because it is supernatural. "And be kind to one another, tenderhearted, forgiving one another, even as God in Christ forgave you" (Ephesians 4:32).

Goodness — God is good, period. He is not evil. Neither should He be blamed for the evil found in the world. This evil is a result of sin and bad choices made by mankind. Goodness is the very nature of God. When God allowed Moses to experience His Presence by passing by him while he stood in the cleft of the rock, the Scripture says that He allowed His "goodness" to pass by (see Exodus 33:19). God's Presence here is described as his "goodness."

Though God is good, yet the Scriptures also tell us that His goodness is to be feared. "Afterward the children of Israel shall return and seek the LORD their God and David their king. They shall fear the LORD and His goodness in the latter days" (Hosea 3:5). This reverent fear keeps us from taking the Lord's goodness for granted.

Because God is good, He is also forgiving: "For You, Lord, are good, and ready to forgive, and abundant in mercy to all those who call upon You" (Psalm 86:5). Because God is good, He also is merciful. "Praise the LORD! Oh, give thanks to the LORD, for He is good! For His mercy endures forever" (Psalm 106:1).

As we abide in the Vine our fruit will also be good. "Every branch in Me that does not bear fruit He takes away; and every branch that bears fruit He prunes, that it may bear more fruit" (John 15:2). We must yield to the Master Gardener and allow Him to prune away any sin in our lives that would yield bad fruit. The goodness of God's Presence must be grown and manifested in our lives.

Jesus is called the "Good Shepherd" and He guards and leads our lives as we follow Him and remain in His Presence. The Good Shepherd's eye is always upon us—His sheep; He watches over us and cares for us. Though we walk through the valley of the shadow of death, as Psalm 23 says, we will not fear any evil for His Presence is with us. Though evil may be present also, yet we do not need to fear it for God's Presence is with us, and He will protect us from any looming evil. The Good Shepherd guides us through the valley of the shadow of death showing us the way to go. Being aware of His Good Presence is what keeps us from the fear of evil and death.

God has a wonderful way of turning bad situations around. "And we know that all things work together for good to those who love God, to those who are the called according to His purpose" (Romans 8:28). Remind yourself of this daily. As you think of God's ability to turn your bad situations around for the good, pray in faith and look to Him for the goodness to surface. Recently my husband and I had a minor situation that looked bad. We took our car in for repair and the mechanic lost our phone number. As a result, he never called us or fixed the car! This looked bad, but as we gave it to the Lord, the mechanic gave us a brand new loaner car while he fixed ours and then took $100.00 off our bill! This is just one minor example of the goodness of God in our lives and the reversal of bad situations. Praise God, He works all things together for the good! His ways are above our ways (see Isaiah 55:8-9). There is no situation that God can't turn around, no heart He can't soften and change. God is good! Because His nature is good, we too must branch out with goodness to others as we abide in Him. "Oh, give thanks to the LORD, for He is good! For His mercy endures forever" (Psalm 118:1).

Faithfulness – God's faithfulness is present in our lives when we abide in Him and His Word. We then become full of faith because "faith comes from hearing, and hearing by the word of God" (Romans 10:17). Being faithful means that we are faithful and true to the One who is our source—the One who is the Giver of all virtues. He is faithful to us first; therefore, we are faithful to Him. Our having faith in God means that we trust God. When we trust God we are faithful to Him. He can be trusted! He is faithful! No one else is faithful 100% of the time. Only God is 100% faithful and true. People all make mistakes and sometimes lose our trust, but God can be trusted. He has proven Himself to us by coming to earth and dying on the cross for our redemption. He saved us; therefore, we can trust Him. Now, because of all He has done for us, we give Him our faithfulness in return.

Our faithfulness needs to be seen in our daily walk by the choices we make. Because we are faithful to God we walk out our faith in obedience to Him. As we abide in His Word, we see how to serve Him in daily life. His Spirit speaks to our hearts and we respond in faithful service. It is then that we can "walk by faith and not by sight," meaning that we are depending upon His faithfulness in our lives (see 2 Corinthians 5:7). Because we are connected to Him—the

Vine—we know that we are safe in His Presence. Our faith in God acts as a shield to us and quenches all the fiery arrows of the evil one that fly by day or by night (see Psalm 91:5; Ephesians 6:16).

Faith is not only a fruit of the Spirit, but also is a gift. It is listed among the manifestation gifts of the Spirit in 1 Corinthians 12:7-12. The gift of faith also works together with miracles. This is because it takes faith to receive miracles and faith to move out in miracles.

"Let us hold fast the confession of our hope without wavering, for He who promised is faithful" (Hebrews 10:23). As we hold fast to our confession of hope in Him, we will be standing in faith and will be faithful to Him. May we all abide in the Vine and receive His grace to be faithful and true to the end. Then we will have the great pleasure of hearing our Lord say, "Well done good and faithful servant ..." (Matthew 25:21, 23). God is faithful and true!

Gentleness— Here the fruit of gentleness is added even though kindness can also be described as gentleness. It is so important that God is restating it. The King James Version translates this word as "meekness." Being meek is a great strength in the Lord, and as the old saying goes, "meekness is not weakness." It is only by yielding our natures to the Spirit of God and abiding in Him that we can be meek and gentle.

All correction needs to be given in a meek spirit and wrapped in as much love and gentleness as possible (see Galatians 6:1; 2 Timothy 2:25). A soft or gentle answer turns away wrath (see Proverbs 15:1). It is a virtue that is ours as we yield to His Spirit and flow in His grace. This virtue is needed in leadership, for we are not to lord it over the sheep but willingly serve them (see 1 Peter 5:3). The great leader Moses was said to be the meekest man in the earth (see Numbers 12:3). Gentleness is a virtue that Apostle Paul instructed Timothy to practice in his leadership also (1 Timothy 6:11). However, Jesus is our greatest example. The Scriptures describe Him as "meek and lowly of heart." Jesus points out His attribute of meekness and then invites us to come and yoke ourselves with Him and learn of His meek ways also (see Matthew 11:29). In learning to practice the meekness of Jesus we reflect His strong yet gentle leadership to others and point to Him. Then others can taste and see that the LORD is good" (Psalm 34:8).

Self-control – The ability to control one's self is an ability that comes by abiding in the Vine of Jesus Christ, for He is the One who gives us the self-control that we need to exercise. The fruit of the Spirit of self-control restrains us from blaming, arguing, and losing our temper. When we break away from Him we find ourselves acting out in fleshly responses. It is only by staying connected to the Vine that we can control ourselves! As we yield to Him, He restrains us. My experience has been that if I inwardly yield my will over to Him, I then receive the grace to control myself and escape from an otherwise explosive reaction that I would soon regret. I have found that it is only in yielding to Him that I am able to let go of the things that I so want to have a fit about. It is our flesh that wants to demand its way and put others in their place, and refraining from doing so gives us time to ask for the wisdom to respond in a godly fashion.

I have heard it said that self-control is like putting a car in "neutral" when we feel like stripping the gears. That is a good picture of self-control. The neutral position is the one to take until we can move ahead in the gear of the Spirit of God. We must disconnect from our emotions and stay connected to Him. As we yield to Him, He gives us the right words, timing, and wisdom to proceed with peace and grace. It is then that the Spirit of God can take control. It is in holding on to Him that we obtain the restraint to hold back our flesh. The flesh can get fired up like a locomotive ready to thrust forward down the wrong track of fury. In doing so, our spirits get railroaded and taken to a place that can only be exited from by the U-turn of repentance and humility. We must get back on the right track, going the right direction, for God cannot trust us to rule in other arenas if we cannot harness our own spirits.

The King James Version translates the word self-control as temperance. When glass is "tempered" it is made stronger so it can uphold under the pressure of heat. God also tempers us by His Spirit so we can be strong when in heated situations. When regular glass is broken it breaks into sharp pointed pieces that can be very dangerous. However, when glass is tempered, it is many times stronger than regular glass; therefore, when broken it shatters into small pieces rather than the jagged, sharp spikes and is less likely to cause injury. God does not want us to have sharp, jagged edges that will inflict pain on others when we are broken. Rather, God desires us to have a broken and contrite heart before Him (see Psalm 51:17). When our plans and dreams are broken, we are to surrender them to Him and refrain from lashing out at others in an attempt to try to get our own way. By allowing Him to "temper" us we become a strong vessel to hold His anointing and grace.

Bear Much Fruit

"But also for this very reason, giving all diligence, add to your faith virtue, to virtue knowledge, to knowledge self-control, to self-control perseverance, to perseverance godliness, to godliness brotherly kindness, and to brotherly kindness love. For if these things are yours and abound, you will be neither barren nor unfruitful in the knowledge of our Lord Jesus Christ" (2 Peter 1:5-8). When we abide in Him—the Vine—we will bear much fruit. The best thing about the nine fruits of the Holy Spirit is they are always in season! We never have to import them from some far-away land, for they are "homegrown" right here in the garden of our own hearts and lives. Others will pick your fruit and be blessed and you will become a fruitful branch.

When spies were sent out to spy out the Promised Land, they returned with the fruit of the land. The Scriptures tell us that the grapes were so large that they had to carry them across huge poles that were carried by two men (see Numbers 13:23). This enormous cluster of grapes is symbolic of the great fruit that we find in His Presence and share with His body of believers and those whom He is calling out. Also, it is symbolic of the fruitfulness of His corporate Presence found as we gather together in Him.

Any fruitful tree is pruned so that it will produce more fruit. We are no different. He is the Vine and we are the branches. It is the branches that need to be pruned. Though it can be rather painful, as we trust the Gardener of our souls, He prunes us back so we will produce yet more fruit for Him. God disciplines those He loves (see Hebrews 12:6). "Now no chastening seems to be joyful for the present, but painful; nevertheless, afterward it yields the peaceable fruit of righteousness to those who have been trained by it" (Hebrews 12:11). Also, God prunes back things in our lives that may get in the way of the fruitful ministry He desires to produce in our lives. He desires our lives to be a ministry unto Him in the area(s) of giftedness that He has appointed us in. Sometimes He will prune back what seems like a fruitful expression of Him, only to later bring us into a greater garden of ministry that is beyond anything we could have hoped for. In this way He widens our fields for His harvest of souls and plantings of righteousness.

Fruit that Remains

When Jesus was baptized, the Scriptures tell us that the Holy Spirit descended upon Him in the form of a dove and *remained* (see John 1:32). In other words, the Holy Spirit did not fly away like doves sometimes do.[1] He remained upon His life. Jesus is our example. We too are to have the Holy Spirit descend upon our lives, and our goal is to have Him remain upon us.

---

1 For more reading on the Spirit descending like a dove see: *The Sensitivity of the Spirit by R.T. Kendall* (Lake Mary, FL: Charisma House), 2002.

This is possible as we abide or remain in Him. In fact, some Bible translations use the word "remain" in place of the word "abide" in regard to our abiding in Christ. When we remain in Him, His Spirit remains upon us. When we lose the fruit of the Holy Spirit in our lives, we become like a thorny bush on which the Dove does not desire to remain perched. Oh, He is still there, but His tangible Presence lifts because His Spirit is grieved:

> And do not grieve the Holy Spirit of God, by whom you were sealed for the day of redemption. Let all bitterness, wrath, anger, clamor, and evil speaking be put away from you, with all malice. And be kind to one another tenderhearted, forgiving one another, even as God in Christ forgave you.
>
> ~ Ephesians 4:30-32 ~

The following chapter then starts out exhorting us to be imitators of God and to walk in love. It then adds that there is not to be even a hint of sexual immorality among us:

> But fornication and all uncleanness or covetousness, let it not even be named among you, as is fitting for saints; neither filthiness, nor foolish talking, nor coarse jesting, which are not fitting, but rather giving of thanks. For this you know, that no fornicator, unclean person, nor covetous man, who is an idolater, has any inheritance

in the kingdom of Christ and God. Let no one deceive you with empty words, for because of these things the wrath of God comes upon the sons of disobedience. Therefore do not be partakers with them.

~ Ephesians 5:3-7 ~

Quite simply, if we are not abiding in Him, if we are not walking in the Spirit of God, then we are walking in the flesh—according to our fleshly nature. The flesh produces the works of the flesh which are in direct opposition to the fruit of the Spirit.

Now the works of the flesh are evident, which are: adultery, fornication, uncleanness, lewdness, idolatry, sorcery, hatred, contentions, jealousies, outbursts of wrath, selfish ambitions, dissensions, heresies, envy, murders, drunkenness, revelries, and the like; of which I tell you beforehand, just as I also told you in time past, that those who practice such things will not inherit the kingdom of God.

~ Galatians 5:19-21 ~

Needless to say practicing such sinful behaviors causes us to lose the Presence of the Spirit upon our lives. You may ask then, "Why do people sometimes operate in the gifts of the Spirit while practicing such deeds? This is quite simply because, "the gifts and the calling of God are irrevocable" (Romans 11:29). The gifts God gives us are just that—*gifts*. He does not take them back. We must practice proper stewardship of them. We will be held accountable as to how we used them and in what spirit we operated them in. It is a sobering thought. Even though operating in the gifts does have a level of the anointing of God upon it (just like the written Word of God has an anointing upon it) we will void the increase of grace and anointing that comes from the tangible Presence of the Spirit of God in our lives and ministry if we are abiding in sin. That is why we can read the Scriptures, preach, prophesy, and even operate in miracles and yet have unrepented sin in our hearts and lives. We must not assume that manifesting the gifts of the Spirit is God's stamp of approval. We shall know them by their fruits (see Matthew 7:16). Likewise, we need both the fruit and the gifts of God in our lives.

> Not everyone who says to Me, 'Lord, Lord,' shall enter the kingdom of heaven, but he who does the will of My Father in heaven. Many will say to Me in that day, 'Lord, Lord, have we not prophesied in Your name, cast out demons in Your name, and done many wonders in Your name?' And then I will declare to them, 'I never knew you; depart from Me, you who practice lawlessness!'

~ Matthew 7:21-23 ~

We cannot abide in sin and in Christ at the same time; it is just not possible, just like you cannot go down two roads simultaneously. This is a sobering thought. It boils down to this: we will be held accountable for our actions and behavior. Our behavior needs to line up with Christ in order to walk with Him. Our relationship with Christ must not be taken for granted, nor neglected.

When we yield to the Spirit of God and when we abide in Him, we remain in Him. It is then that we exhibit the fruitfulness of that abiding relationship. It is then that His Spirit empowers us to live a holy life. It is then that we become a fruitful branch for His Spirit to remain rested upon. It is then that our ministry is truly anointed. When we die to our own selfish desires and respond to others in a godly, loving manner, we exhibit the fruitfulness of God. It is then that the anointing that can only come from His Presence is seen upon our lives and ministry. And it is by remaining in Him that His fruit will remain in our lives. Jesus said, "You did not choose Me, but I chose you and appointed you that your fruit should *remain* ..." (John 15:16, emphasis mine). It is then that we will be known by our fruits.

Prayer

Lord, you are the Vine, I but a mere humble branch. I can do nothing without You. I abide in You and partake of the goodness that flows forth from You. I choose to remain in You and yield to You, even in times of spiritual pruning. Flow through me I pray and bring forth the luscious fruit of love, joy, peace, longsuffering, kindness, goodness, faithfulness, gentleness, and self-control. Help me to yield to You and to be a fruitful branch for you to dwell upon. Bring increase in the fruitfulness and anointing of my ministry for You, and allow me to plant seeds in the lives and hearts of others all for your glory and the increase of Your heavenly garden. In Jesus' Name I pray. Amen.

CHAPTER 7

—§—

His Glorious Presence

Can a virgin forget her ornaments,
or a bride her attire? Yet My people have
forgotten Me
days without number.

~ JEREMIAH 2:32 ~

GOD CREATED MAN and woman in His own image and likeness.
He loved them, He walked and talked with them in the cool
of the day, and He gave them His whole world. The whole
world was created for His children to enjoy. In His beautiful
Garden that He planted for his children, He placed Adam, His
first created one. He took him on a walk of his new home,
this garden paradise, and as they strolled along in the cool of
the day, He pointed out each of the beautiful fruit trees He
had planted there. He explained that they were all there for
his enjoyment, with one exception—the tree of the knowledge
of good and evil. That one was not to be eaten of, for it was
deadly. Woman was created out of man by God both in His

image and likeness, and they became a beautiful team for God tending the Garden together.

The man and woman were not the only ones in the Garden, however, for an enemy lurked in the shadows—a deceiver who desired to strip this godly couple of their godly attire. But how? How could he steal from them? How could he make them fall? He presented the twisted truth to the woman that the barred tree held the benefit of giving them the incredible knowledge of good and evil so they could be like God, and the only reason God didn't want them to eat of it was because He didn't want them to be like Him. The woman believed this lie. She failed to recognize that they were already made in God's image and likeness; therefore, they *were already* like Him. She ate of the tree's fruit and gave it to her husband who partook of it willingly while both ignored its grave side-effect—*death*.

Immediately after partaking of this forbidden fruit, it yielded its results, for this once godly couple now stood naked while, at the same time, their eyes were opened to this horrific result. Naked and ashamed, they sewed together fig leaves to cover themselves while being quick to hide from the voice of the Lord. The Lord missed their presence, so He visited them with His. He called out to them in the Garden, "Adam where are you?" Adam responded that he heard Him calling, but they hid because they were naked. The Lord asked them if they had eaten of the forbidden fruit, and the man said yes that they had but was quick to blame his wife for inviting him to do so. God confronted the woman, who quickly responded that the serpent had deceived her into doing so.

Why did Adam and Eve scurry around in a desperate attempt to cover their nakedness? Why were they ashamed of their nakedness? Were they previously naked and yet unashamed? Were they not created naked? Were their eyes not just now opened to this fact because they ate of the fruit of good and evil?

The truth is … Adam and Eve had lost their covering. They were not created naked and left naked. God did not let them run around without a covering. *No. He Himself was their covering.* He covered them … *with His Glory!*

When they sinned, they lost their covering—they lost the Glory. Then they stood naked and ashamed. They were stripped of their Glory. Their eyes were opened to this fact as well. Both of these results—as well as spiritual and eventual physical death—came from eating of the tree of the knowledge of good and evil—the forbidden fruit. After the Lord explained the cursed results of the couple's transgression, the Lord God made clothing for them that was more suitable than fig leaves from the tunics of animal skins (see Gen 3:21).

The Cover-Up

After losing the Glory—their covering—they stood naked, and their eyes now became opened to understand this evil they had done; they scurried around frantically to cover up. Then they hid from the Presence of God. How like them we all are! We take His Glory for granted. Or perhaps we have never experienced it. Either way—we stand naked. The enemy of our souls has deceived and tempted us to compromise our faith and to transgress against the Lord. The Glory of His Presence dissolves in the midst of sin, leaving us naked. Our nakedness causes shame. Our shame causes us to want to cover up. We look around frantically for something to cover up with. Like Adam and Eve, we try to camouflage ourselves with the coverings of the world around us. We try to blend in with everyone else, and sadly, we do.

Sometimes we try to cover up with good works. We try to cover our sin by doing a good work like volunteering for a community event, or giving money to charity, or something else that will make us feel good. But these are merely earthly coverings. We may have a form of godliness, but are void of the glory of God.

Our sin causes us to lose His Glory—His glorious Presence—that He desires to cover us with, His glorious Presence that He wants us to wear like a garment, His glorious Presence that He desires to shine from our person, His glorious Presence that illuminates our oneness with Him. His glorious Presence has been traded for mere worldly garments.

> But My people have changed their Glory
> for what does not profit.
>
> ~ JEREMIAH 2:11 ~

We trade in our glorious robes of righteousness for filthy rags of compromise and empty good works. It's like trading in a kingly robe for a mere garage sale garment. Whenever we sin, whenever we compromise the things of God in disobedience, it's like we are stripped naked! Then we wear rags of sin. Generally, when one is found naked they become embarrassed—ashamed of it; however, sometimes not. Sometimes we are not ashamed to wear our dirty attire. Being ashamed of our sin is the best thing that could happen, for when we feel ashamed and are convicted of our sin, we then can be moved to call upon the Lord to forgive us of our sin and to cover us again. If this does not occur, we then try to cover up with our own good works. The Bible tells us that our own good works are as "filthy rags" (see Isaiah 64:6). When we cover up with the attitudes of the world and mere good works we blend in. We should not blend in but stand out! We need to wear His Glory and shine His Glory!

Why would we want to trade the Glory of the Lord for mere rags? Some have never worn the Glory. Some are wearing rags of shame—ashamed of the things done in the past. Shame is attached to you like a skin-tight body suit. You have become one with it, but Christ wants to peel off the sin and the shame that accompanies it and cover you with His Glory—His glorious Presence.

Change Clothes

Wearing the same old clothes day after day causes them to become soiled and tattered. Their rough woven fabrics rub against our spirits like a rough woolen sweater. We are in need of a spiritual change of clothes daily, even several times a day. The Bible tells us to "put off" our old clothing that is made of man-made fabrics of: lust, lying, stealing, corrupt words, bitterness, hatred, slander, quarreling, abusive language, spite, ill-will, covetousness, fornication, and foolish talking (see Ephesians 4:20-5:5). The wearing of these garments wears thin in the Presence of God.

"Layering" clothes is popular both for fashion reasons and climate reasons. Spiritually, some of us have layers and layers of clothing we have covered up with, yet we still feel naked—ashamed. That is because another layer of clothing will not help. It only will make us yet more uncomfortable and unsatisfied. We are all in need of a heavenly garment—the garment of His Presence. However, God will not put a layer of His Glory over T-shirts of iniquity. The warmth of His Presence will not come to hard, cold, unforgiving hearts. He will not cover our garments of sin unless we are willing to take them off. We must be willing to take off the old garment—our old ways of dealing with life, before He will clothe us with His Presence. Once we take off the old, once we confess our old covering as sin and ask for His forgiveness and grace to do things His way, then His Presence falls like a sheet of grace and He wraps Himself around us like a warm blanket. Then we feel the warmth of His embrace. Then we are secure under the protection of His wrap. Then our shame is gone and we are robed in His righteousness. "But put on the Lord Jesus Christ, and make no provision for the flesh, to fulfill its lusts" (Romans 13:14).

Stealing Your Shirt

The enemy of our souls is out to steal our shirts! He wants to rob us of our covering. He wants us to lose the glorious covering of the Lord's Presence. It's easy to do so. It is as easy as leaving your jacket in someone's car. We go on our merry way and as soon as the climate changes and it becomes a bit cold, we realize that we forgot our coat. How does it happen? We get preoccupied with life and just doing things in the natural and before you know it, we are wrapped in rags and realize that we lost our shirts! The phrase "lost your shirt" is a phrase that refers to losing all your money. But in this case it is not mere money that we have lost, but His Glory—the mark of real spiritual poverty.

The enemy who was active in the beginning trying to cause the first man and woman to lose their heavenly attire is still at work in our daily lives to tempt and trick us into losing our glorious covering.

Keep Your Shirt On

In the olden days, men used to take off their shirts before engaging in a fight. Thus the saying, "keep your shirt on" came into being. It means to be patient, keep calm, and avoid fighting. The same can be said spiritually. Once we lose our patience, begin quarreling, and get a bad attitude we find that we no longer are wearing the Glory. We must learn to "keep our shirts on."

We see in His Word how to "keep our shirt on" spiritually: "Do not lie to one another, since you have put off the old man with his deeds, and have put on the new man who is renewed in knowledge according to the image of Him who created him" and "Therefore, as the elect of God, holy and beloved, put on tender mercies, kindness, humility, meekness, longsuffering; bearing with one another, and forgiving one another, if anyone has a complaint against another; even as Christ forgave you, so you also must do. But above all these things put on love, which is the bond of perfection" (Colossians 3:9-10, 12-14). These verses tell us how to keep our heavenly attire on. When we die to self and yield to the Spirit of God by not losing our cool with others, when we sacrificially suffer for Him, when we reach out in love rather than strike back in anger, and we do it for Him, He wraps His Presence around us. It is then that we sense His Presence and wear Him like a garment. There is nothing I would rather wear.

The Blood Precedes the Glory

After Adam and Eve sinned and were found naked and ashamed before the Lord in the Garden, the Scriptures tell us that God Himself made for them coverings from animal skins. This was in fact the first blood sacrifice (see Genesis 3:21). Later, God instructs the Israelites about the need of the shedding of blood to forgive sins, and He initiates the blood sacrifice for the (temporary) forgiveness of sin. Jesus, however, became the final sacrifice for our sins. He was the Lamb that was slain from the foundation of the world (see Revelation 13:8).

With that initial blood sacrifice in the Garden, God was pointing to the coming of Jesus, the Lamb of God, which would be the final sacrifice for our sins. The blood of the animals had to be shed before the skins could cover Adam and Eve as clothing. Likewise, we cannot be covered with His glorious Presence without first coming under the forgiving power of

His blood. The Blood precedes the Glory. As we come to Him with continuous, repentant hearts, bowing our hearts before Him daily in continuous surrender, giving Him our sin and weakness, and relying on Him for His power and strength, He then lets His glorious Presence fall upon us. He then wraps us in His Glory.

Weights of Glory

Clothing comes in different weights. For example, you can have a pair of blue jeans that are made of thin denim, and a pair that is made of thick denim. They both are denim blue jeans but their weights are different. The same goes for any piece of clothing. You might have a wool jacket that is light and another heavy woolen jacket. The thicker the fabric the heavier it is.

The Hebrew word that is used to speak of the Glory of God's Presence also means "weight". His Presence is weighty, and comes upon us much like clothing—in different weights. Elijah had one weight of Glory and Elisha had another. Actually, Elisha had *double* of the weight of Glory. The Hebrew word used for Elijah's mantle also means glory. Elisha told Elijah that he desired to have a double portion of this glorious anointing that was upon Elijah's life and ministry. Elijah told Elisha that if he were to witness his being taken up to Heaven by the Lord, he would get his heart's desire. Elisha stayed with Elijah and witnessed the whirlwind of the Lord take Elijah up. Then Elijah's mantle fell from Heaven and was picked up by Elisha (see 2 Kings 2:1-14). Elisha then walked in a double portion of the anointing that was upon Elijah's life. As a result, Elisha operated in double the miracles that Elijah did.

We too can have a mantle from the Lord. The weight of the mantle depends upon our calling and our response to that calling. It also depends upon our relationship with the Lord and how we maintain that relationship. The closer the relationship is—the weightier the mantle of Glory. The mantle is kept by keeping up a close and intimate relationship with Him. We must stay with Him and be sensitive to Him. We must realize immediately if we do anything to grieve or quench His Spirit and repent of it immediately.

Elisha asked for a double portion. We too must not be afraid to ask for more. Ask for a greater portion of His Spirit. Ask for a double portion. Believe to walk in the miraculous. Expect God to use you.

A greater mantle of Glory means a greater responsibility. The anointing gets heavy, in a good sense, but heavy nevertheless. We must develop the character and stamina needed to be able to carry the weight of it. Tests will come, but tests show us what we are made of. Be willing to endure the tests and be determined to pass them. Do it all to please Him, and He will delight in you. Delight means favor, and favor gets you a thicker mantle of His Glory.

Joseph in the Old Testament was one who had great favor in the eyes of his father, Jacob. Jacob in turn gave Joseph a "coat of many colors." This coat was a covering of honor. His brothers were jealous of his coat and stripped him of it (see Genesis 37:3,

23). Then they threw him into a pit. Joseph then was sold into slavery and taken to Egypt. He had to pass many tests in order to come into his calling. Joseph passed his tests and ended up being the second most powerful leader in all of Egypt. Likewise, God our Father looks favorably upon His sons and daughters who aim to please Him. He places a beautiful coat of Glory upon us. We must wear it humbly and wisely. And we must be willing to go through any tests that may come our way to come into our realms of service that the Lord has for us.

It is all for His Glory! That phrase has two meanings: First, it is all to be clothed in His glorious Presence. Secondly, it is all done to bring glory to Him! When we keep this perspective and endure hardship for Him, He will bless us with His Presence and take us into our destiny. To Him be all the glory, for He indeed is Glorious!

Prayer

Lord Jesus, I desire to be clothed in Your Presence. I long to wear Your Glory. Please forgive me for every sin and offense that has stripped me of the Glory that You desire me to be wrapped in. Nothing is worth losing Your Presence over. No resentment, no worldly desire, no frustration is worth losing Your marvelous Glory over. Please forgive me. I repent of every bad thought and action. I repent for doing things that I shouldn't have done and for not doing things that I should have. Forgive me for trying to cover up with other things.

Please wrap me again afresh in Your glorious Presence. I ask even for a double portion of the anointing. Help me to build my character so I can carry the weight of Your Glory. Let me walk in more. I desire to do the works You have for me to do and to walk in the power of Your Presence. Come and clothe me with Your Glory! Amen.

CHAPTER 8

—— § ——

Coming Out to Enter into His Presence

When Israel went out of Egypt,
the house of Jacob from a people of strange
language,
Judah became His sanctuary,
and Israel His dominion.

~ PSALM 114:1-2 ~

WHEN ISRAEL WENT out of Egypt, they came into a new place in God. He became their sanctuary; they came into His Presence. God called Israel out of Egypt—out of bondage. It was there, in Egypt, that God's people were enslaved to heavy bondage. Therefore, Egypt is a type of sin and bondage. It is a metaphor for us. As God sent Moses to deliver the Israelites out of their bondage, He sent Jesus to save us out of ours! Jesus is our Savior; He is our Deliverer! When we were saved, Jesus, our Deliverer, called us out. He called us out of the darkness and into His marvelous light. We heard His voice calling, and we answered Him. There are, however, other times the Lord calls us out.

The Fresh Call

Today, there is a fresh calling from the Spirit of God. If you remember, there was a time when Egypt was a blessing for the people of Israel. It was when Jacob and his sons were experiencing a famine, God sent Joseph ahead of them to Egypt. This sending was a bit out of the ordinary, for his brothers actually sold him into bondage. Nevertheless, Joseph himself later recognized that it was God who sent him ahead of them for the purpose of blessing them and providing for them. Joseph became the most powerful one in Egypt, next to Pharaoh himself, and was able to bless his family. So, Jacob and his sons moved to Egypt and settled in the land of Goshen. There they grew and multiplied and became very blessed. However, in time, a new Pharaoh arose who did not know Joseph nor did he have any regard for the Israelites. So, he oppressed them greatly with slave labor (see Genesis 37; 41-47; Exodus 1:8-11). Then God set apart His servant Moses and called him to lead His people out of Egypt. God always makes a way of escape for us.

There is a fresh calling. God is calling us out from the place in which we have become familiar. Did you know that the Israelites had become accustomed to Egypt? Yes, even with the cruel bondage they were accustomed to it. It had become familiar. How do I know? Because, later, when they were out of their comfort zone and had to trust God, they wanted to return. They craved the leeks and onions the Bible tells us. They craved the familiar (see Numbers 11:4-6). God is calling us out of the familiar and into a new place—a place of trusting Him. Though it may have been a blessing, He does not want it to become our sanctuary. For any other sanctuary—any other place we put our trust in—but Him is indeed an idol.

God has called me out from familiar places. I was once employed by a major corporation for many years that was a great financial blessing for my family. The income allowed us to put our two boys through Bible school. However, the time came when God called me out. I too, like the Israelites, was forced to make bricks without straw! Ha Ha! But I always said, "It was God who put me there and it will be God who takes me out." I stayed there until God called me out.

When making a big decision like quitting your job you want to make sure it is God. You want confirmations and godly council. You want to hear from God and then submit what you are hearing to your spiritual coverings and make sure you are hearing correctly. If it is God, many things will line up and there will be coherence. I felt God was calling me out of my corporate employment, but I wasn't sure where He was calling me to. I was like Abraham being called out to be a blessing, but not knowing where I was going. I thought that God was going to get me a new job, and there was a place that I wanted to be hired, so I was praying for doors to open there and for the new job to come before I left the old. It only seemed logical to have a new job lined up before leaving the old. However, God does not always fit our logic. Sometimes He is beyond logic, and sometimes He requires us to take a step or leap of faith. God was calling me to leave the old before the new opened up!

I was receiving prophetic words from my covering with Christian International that God was calling me out. My pastor agreed also that I was probably to leave my job, but he said that I needed to really know, and that I wasn't there yet. My husband agreed that I could leave, but he wanted me to get my two weeks' vacation time in first. So, I really sought the Lord for a Word. I said, "Lord, I need a Word to stand on, so I will not *waver*." I really needed to know. I needed that Word to stand on. When making a big decision, you have to know that you know that you know. So I set my face like flint to seek the Lord. The Lord then spoke to me that He was calling me out from my job to write another book. He said, "You fear loss, but the greater loss will come when you get here and find all the work here that you have not finished." Then He said that I could say that I work for Him now. Now that's a fresh call!

I said Ok God, I will prepare to quit. But then, I let my mind go back to the other thing—to other job postings, etc. Did you ever do that? Did you ever make a decision and then begin to think about the opposite again? The Bible tells us in James 1:8 that a double minded man is unstable in all his ways. I began to think about some other job postings at work that I was interested in, and I began to think about applying for those positions. Then the Lord invaded my thoughts by striking me with a sharp Word. (You know the kind that divides the soul from spirit?) He said, *"How long will you waver between two decisions?"*

That word really struck me! I recognized it as a Scripture verse, but wasn't sure where it was. I knew it was nothing I had read recently. So, when I got to work, I googled it. It was taken from Elijah's encounter when upon Mount Carmel when he spoke to the crowd of people and said, "… How long will you *waver* between two opinions? If the Lord is God, follow him; but if Baal is God, follow him" (1 Kings 18:21 NIV, emphasis mine). I knew through that Word that God was also saying to me, "You cannot serve both God and mammon" (Luke 16:13). Yes, my job—money—had become a "god" to me. Being convicted in my heart, I made the final and determined decision that I would quit my job. I prepared to exit by taking my two weeks' paid vacation prior to giving my two weeks' notice. This I felt was acceptable to the Lord.

When the Lord calls us to change, we must make the quality decision to follow Him. It is necessary to know for sure it is the Lord, but once we have determined that it is God, we must then follow completely—without hesitation. There can be no straddling the fence, no one foot in our own camp and one foot in God's. We must make a move and be planted in God's will. We must set our face like flint and not be moved. We cannot allow our minds to entertain thoughts of spiritual infidelity. We must follow Him completely and come out from our comfort zone. I had asked the Lord for a Word to stand on that I may not *waiver*. The word "waiver" was actually in the striking Word that He had spoken to me for He asked me how long I would "waiver" between two decisions. God is awesome! He always meets us where we are and speaks into our very being. He chooses His Words exactly. His Word shakes the cedars (see Psalm 29:5-11)! When we have a Word to stand on and mix the Word with faith, we can stand through all adversity.

Oh, Those Leeks and Onions!

Now, Satan, the enemy of our souls, does not want you to obey God. He does not want you to move on to your promised land! No, Pharaoh did not want to let God's people go! He pursued them. So also the enemy will pursue us when we are following God, and if one thing doesn't work, he will try another.

When I decided to leave my job, my boss called me over to his desk and gave me a great review (unlike any I had ever received before)! He then gave me a raise, and made it retroactive for three months back pay! Oh, those leeks and onions! Just like the Israelites were called out and then were tempted to return by the thought of the leeks and onions they ate while in Egypt, so I also was feeling the temptation to remain in the land of bondage (see Numbers 11:4-6; 1 Corinthians 10:6).

No temptation has overtaken you except such as is common to man; but God is faithful, who will not allow you to be tempted beyond what you are able, but with the temptation will also make the way of escape, that you may be able to bear it.

~ 1 Corinthians 10:13 ~

We must resist the temptations. We resist with the Word of the Lord. God had given me a Word to stand on, so I would not waiver anymore! I put the word on my computer, and I deleted the emails of the new job postings. Sometimes the temptations persist. Satan does not want us to move with God's cloud of Presence. He wants us to stay in the old bondage. When God's cloud moves, we must move. If we stay in the old place we will be in bondage! It may have been a blessing before, but it will no longer be. When God's Glory lifts off something, we must leave it—if it's Biblical. God isn't going to tell you to leave your spouse for the attractive person down the road. No, that's not God. Nor is He going to tell you to desert your children. No, that's not God. He isn't going to tell you to leave church and stay at home isolated. No, that's not God. Make sure it is Biblical. ... Amen? But when God says to leave the old place, leave it. Obey God and be blessed with His Presence that will accompany you.

More temptation came for me. The day before I left for my two weeks paid vacation, another manager within the company found me and tried to hire me in his department saying, "Oh, but Kathy, you would be perfect for the job!" See, when more money doesn't work, the enemy will try praise and flattery; he appeals to our pride. But we must obey God! So I resisted the temptation, and said, "No, God is calling me to quit and write another book." You see, in resisting the temptation, God will use you to testify about Him. In your resistance, you will be pointing the way to Jesus. Your life will be an example.

My husband, Mike, and I went on our wonderful two weeks' vacation to Florida and then to Nassau. When I returned, I went into work to give my two weeks' notice (however, when you give two weeks' notice there, they walk you out to your car and you are done, so I was prepared for that). I told the Lord, "Lord, if you open the door for me, I will give them the Gospel." So when I handed in my letter of resignation, my two managers asked me to come over to their desk. They asked me to just talk to them and tell them why I was going. So I did; I gave them Scripture verses and all! Then my manager asked, "Well, is He saying anything to the two of us?" WHAT AN OPEN DOOR! So I said, "As a matter of fact He is!" Then I was able to lay out the Gospel for them, and make it personal for them. It was a great seed planting time, and a time of speaking for the Lord. God made a good and godly exit.

Leave Well

When we leave the old place, we don't have to leave badly. We don't have to leave in anger and bitterness. We don't have to leave people wounded and hurt. No, we can leave and should leave *godly*. Leave pointing the way to Jesus. Leave a deposit of God's grace behind! If at all possible, leave well. Leave being an example, leave them talking good about you, and leave them thinking about God. "If it is possible, as much as depends on you, live peaceably with all men" (Romans 12:18). " Pursue peace with all people, and holiness, without which no one will see the Lord: looking carefully lest anyone fall short of the grace of God; lest any root of bitterness springing up cause trouble, and by this many become defiled" (Hebrews 12:14-15).

When we are done with something in our society, we just throw it away. We throw out containers of all sorts; even small appliances that used to be repaired are now thrown away because it is more cost effective to simply buy a new one. However, when leaving old places, we most times are leaving relationships behind as well. Even if God is moving us on, we still have a responsibility to leave those relationships well. People matter. Leave well. It's not just how we *start* that matters but how we *finish.*

Overcoming Guilt

Sometimes when God is calling us out of the old place, we have to overcome the guilt of leaving. This guilt is not justified. If God is moving us on then we do not need to feel guilty. Guilt is a shame we feel for doing wrong. However, when no wrong is being done, the guilt is not justified. It is in fact a *false guilt.* Therefore, we can cast it off like an old garment.

If we will look underneath the guilt, however, we will find that it is based in *fear.* We feel guilty for leaving because we really don't trust that God will take care of that in which we are leaving or that He will not take care of those being affected by the move. But we can trust God! He has a plan, and although He may not be disclosing the details of that plan to you, He can be trusted. After you have fulfilled your obligations (and we should fulfill our obligations, since that is part of leaving well), know that God will take care of that in which you are leaving and those affected by the move. Do not hang onto the old thing out of false guilt and fear. Move on, and put it in His hands.

Remaining Distinctive

Psalm 114:1 describes the place in which the Israelites were leaving: "When Israel went out of Egypt, The house of Jacob *from a people of strange language*... (emphasis mine)." They were in the midst of a people of strange language. In other words, they did not learn the language of Egypt. They kept their native tongue. They kept their distinctiveness. People, God is calling us to keep our distinctiveness, no matter where we are! We are in the world and not of it! The twelfth chapter of Romans, verse two tells us not to be conformed to the image of this world, but to be transformed by the renewing of our minds. We renew our minds by feeding on His daily manna that only He can provide— His daily bread. He changes us. We aren't supposed to look like the world. We are the salt of the earth and the light also, for the light of Christ is to shine through us. And we are to spice up the world we live in by our saltiness, and we are to preserve or keep those around us through the love and power of Christ.

But what happens? We can get sucked into the world like a vacuum. If we are not maintaining our distinction, we will learn the language of the world. One compromise can lead to another and another. And before you know it we are talking the talk of the world. We are hiding out amongst the fig leaves of the world covering up with the camouflage of the world—trying to "blend in." We are not called to blend in people! Sin causes us to hide and try to cover up. We cover up with the world's covering; we try to blend in with the common folk—camouflaging ourselves. But it won't work. Why? We have been *called out* by God. "Adam? Where are you?" (Genesis 3:9, paraphrased). Our caring Heavenly Father, who so desires to walk with us in the cool of the day, calls us out! 2 Corinthians 6:17 tells us to "Come out from among them and be separate" in behavior. We must come to an end of our ways and do things His way. He is the Way. Our way includes: impure living, serving others' ungodly needs in exchange for our own needs and desires being met, control and manipulation, driving forces of selfish ambition and jealousy, fits of anger and bullying to get one's way, turning to drugs, abuse of prescription drugs and alcohol, wild parties, bar hopping, and other similar things (see Galatians 5:19-21). These are old ways that only lead us back to the land of bondage. Love the sinner, but hate the sin. Don't do as they do and don't talk as they talk. Arise and shine for Him.

God's Territory

When we come out, when we come out from worldliness, when we come out from our sin, out from our bondage, out from that which God is calling us out from, out from the old …"Judah became His sanctuary, and Israel His dominion" (Psalm 114:2). The land given to the tribe of Judah ended up becoming the location of the Temple. It was built there in Jerusalem. And Israel became God's dominion—His territory.

When we come out in obedience to Him, His Spirit resides with us! We are His dwelling place: Zion—the perfection of beauty, where God shines forth (Psalm 50:2)! We are the temple of the Most High God! He dwells within us! Glory!!! What an honor! What a privilege to be the house of God to carry Him to the world!

When we come out, we meet up with God for He goes before us. His Spirit then rests upon us, and He dwells in our midst! We, the people of God, are filled with His Spirit as we yield in obedience to His leadings and His biddings. We must come out in order to enter in. When His cloud and fire move on, we must follow, for to stay behind is to dwell in darkness, confusion, and bondage. Follow His lead. Follow His Presence.

Prayer

Lord, give me strength to follow You wherever You lead. Give me the faith I need to respond to Your bidding. Help me to leave behind everything that You are calling me out from that I may dwell with You, and You with me. To be in Your perfect will is where I want to be. Help me to leave well and to trust You with the details in Jesus' Name. Amen.

In His Presence

He brought you out of Egypt with His Presence, with His mighty power, driving out from before you nations greater and mightier than you, *to bring you in*, to give you their land as an inheritance, as it is this day.

~ Deuteronomy 4:37b-38 (emphasis mine) ~

CHAPTER 9

Miracles in His Presence

Tremble, O earth, at the presence
of the Lord,
at the presence of the God of Jacob,
who turned the rock into a pool of water,
the flint into a fountain of waters.

~ PSALMS 114:7-8 ~

GOD IS CALLING us to come up higher—into His Presence.
My husband, Mike, loves to hike the Adirondack Mountains
of New York. Over past years, I have gotten in shape enough
to join him in some of these adventures. The view from the
summits can be breathtaking! Other times, when we reach the
summit, we find ourselves immersed in a cloud. When this
occurs, we can see nothing but the mist around us. That is
how it is with God also. He desires to take us up higher in

Him. There are times when we come into His Presence that He shows us wonderful things, and there are times when His Presence engulfs us like a cloud. When His Glory surrounds us we are totally captivated with Him. He is all we see.

When Jesus walked the earth, He invited His disciples Peter, James, and John to accompany Him in a hike up a mountain. When they reached the top, they, too, were engulfed in a cloud—the cloud of God's Presence. Then they heard the Father's voice say, "This is My beloved Son, in whom I am well pleased. Hear Him!" (Matthew 17:5). We also, are to come up higher with Him, and when we do, we also can experience His glory cloud and hear His voice. During such times, He is all we see. We become totally immersed in His Presence.

In Old Testament times, after the completion of the tabernacle, the Scriptures tell us that the cloud of God's Glory filled the tabernacle. Moses was not even able to enter the tabernacle because the Glory of the Lord was so strong (see Exodus 40:34-35). Again, after the completion of Solomon's temple, the people offered up praise and thanksgiving to the Lord, and the Ark of God's Presence was brought in. Then the cloud of God's Presence came and filled the temple. His Presence was so strong that the priest could not even stand to minister (see 1 Kings 8:1-13; 2 Chronicles 5:2-14).

God desires to dwell with His people. The Hebrew word for Glory is *Shekinah* and it means to dwell. There are times when He chooses to display His *Shekinah* Glory to us. When He displays His Glory, we sense His Presence around us. Sometimes His Presence is so strong that we, like the priest of old, can no longer stand but are overcome by His Presence. We fall to our knees in worship of Him! This can happen while in an anointed church service, but it also can happen while we are alone with Him and call upon His Presence. I have had experiences with the Lord that have taken me to my knees and overwhelmed me so as I could no longer stand. I have even had an experience of being literally "glued" to the floor as He demonstrated His Powerful Presence! These wonderful times with the Lord are possible as we worship Him and wait upon His Presence. This is miraculous.

Favor in the Presence of the King

The ruling power in a monarchy is the king or queen. Important changes within the kingdom are only made possible through the decree of the monarchy. The favor and presence of the crown was sought by people who were moved to bring about change for the benefit of the people of their kingdom. If the individual found favor with the monarchy, their voice would be heard and their request granted.

During Old Testament times, Esther was one who had great favor with the king. She went before the king to ask a request. The king looked favorably upon her and as she approached him on his throne, he extended his golden scepter which was a sign of favor. He then requested her anything she wanted even up to half of his kingdom! Esther petitioned the king regarding the fatal future of the Jewish people. Esther found favor and her request was granted while in the presence of the king. Esther's people were saved from their destruction (see Esther 5-8).

Nehemiah was another one who found great favor with the king. He served as cupbearer to a Persian king. Nehemiah was in the king's presence as he served him. The king noticed that something was troubling Nehemiah and asked him what it was. Nehemiah told the king how he had heard that his people back in Jerusalem were in great anguish from the captivity that had occurred there and that the wall of the city was burned and broken down. The king was moved and, therefore, granted Nehemiah permission to return to Jerusalem where he was appointed governor. He and the Jewish people rebuilt the city wall (see Nehemiah 1-6). Favor was found in the presence of the king.

The same holds true for us today. We must bring our request for change before the King of Kings. Miracles can only take place as they are granted by Him. We must come before His Presence. A miracle is an event that is not brought about by scientific or natural means and can only occur by the power of God. As we come into His Presence, He hears our request and our faith gets His attention. Coming worshipfully and reverently before His throne moves the heart of God.

Our motive to come into His Presence is to enjoy Him. He longs to be with us. Yet, it is during these special times with Him that we should also remember to make our request known to Him. Petition Him in prayer while He is manifesting His Presence. Cry out to Him while His Presence is being felt and demonstrated. "Seek the Lord while He may be found, call upon Him while He is near" (Isaiah 55:6).

I have had times while in God's Presence that He has granted my heart's desires and my prayerful request. He perfects that which concerns us (see Psalm 138:8). God has healed me from allergies, anxiety, headaches, and more. My fears melt away while in His Presence. Faith arises while in His Presence. It is then that miracles are made possible.

While in the Presence of the King of Kings, He also makes known what His will is and how He desires to use us to minister to others and to expand His Kingdom. Wisdom is found while in His Presence. It is in His Presence that He shares His heart and mind with us. While in His Presence, He downloads His plan for us to go out and reach our world. We then can decree and proclaim His Word bringing change, for He watches over His Word to perform it (see Jeremiah 1:12). As faith arises, we then proclaim His Word and step out to pray for others' miracles. He calls us to a higher way—miracles included!

Miracles Released

In the beginning, we find the Holy Spirit hovering or brooding over the face of the waters (see Genesis 1:2). Hens brood over their eggs and new life springs forth. Likewise, the Holy Spirit hovered over, or brooded over, the face of the waters to bring forth the creations that God spoke forth. In like manner, The Spirit of God hovers and broods over us and our situations in order to birth something new in and through us. As we stay beneath His Presence and declare His Word as prompted by His Spirit, miracles are released and new, abundant life springs forth!

Desire Miracles

At the church where I minister, one of my jobs is training, activating, and imparting spiritual gifts to the people. When teaching on the manifestation gifts—word of wisdom, word of knowledge, faith, healing, miracles, prophecy, discernment of spirits, tongues, and interpretation (see 1 Corinthians 12:4-11), I like to ask a new group for a show of hands to see who moves in what. Miracles are always way down on the list (if not non-existent); nevertheless, it is a gift given by His Spirit for the demonstration of His power to His people. He desires to manifest His power not only *to* you, but also *through* you!

Many times while teaching and activating spiritual gifts, I use a spiritual gifts assessment test to help people to see what it is they are operating in. I like Peter Wagner's test because it includes dozens of possible spiritual gifts for God's people to identify, so everyone finds they are currently operating in *something*. However, I always tell people not to think that is all they get, for the Word of God tells us to earnestly desire His spiritual gifts (see 1 Corinthians 12:31; 14:1). He gives them as He determines, but we are to desire them earnestly. If we are doing our part, then we will be asking Him for spiritual gifts and desiring for Him to use us to help others. The Word also tells us to especially desire the best gifts or greater gifts (see 1 Corinthians 12:31). Miracles are a greater gift and I believe that is exactly why most people *do not* earnestly desire it. The average Christian thinks they are not spiritual enough for such a great gift and, therefore, they would never think of asking for it. Oh, they may ask God for a miracle, but they wouldn't dare ask Him to use them as an instrument to bring the miracle to pass. If a miracle is to happen they tell themselves, then it will have to be as God brings it to pass—sovereignly. While God may very well show forth His miraculous power sovereignly, He also desires to show Himself strong through you and me—His body here on the earth. His eyes are forever combing the earth—looking for ones in whom He can show Himself strong (see 2 Chronicles 16:9). He looks for vessels to flow through in all the manifestation gifts *including miracles.*

Other times people have been taught a cessationist viewpoint that says the manifestation gifts have ceased to exist. This teaching is based on a false interpretation of 1 Corinthians 13:8-13.These verses are taken out of context and misinterpreted to say that the gifts have now ceased. Let's take a look at these verses in their context:

> Though I speak with the tongues of men and of angels, but have not love, I have become sounding brass or a clanging cymbal. And though I have the gift of prophecy, and understand all mysteries and all knowledge, and though I have all faith, so that I could remove mountains, but have not love, I am nothing. And

though I bestow all my goods to feed the poor, and though I give my body to be burned, but have not love, it profits me nothing.

Love suffers long and is kind; love does not envy; love does not parade itself, is not puffed up; does not behave rudely, does not seek its own, is not provoked, thinks no evil; does not rejoice in iniquity, but rejoices in the truth; bears all things, believes all things, hopes all things, endures all things.

Love never fails. But whether there are prophecies, they will fail; whether there are tongues, they will cease; whether there is knowledge, it will vanish away. For we know in part and we prophesy in part. But when that which is perfect has come, then that which is in part will be done away.

When I was a child, I spoke as a child, I understood as a child, I thought as a child; but when I became a man, I put away childish things. For now we see in a mirror, dimly, but then face to face. Now I know in part, but then I shall know just as I also am known.

And now abide faith, hope, love, these three; but the greatest of these is love.

~ 1 Corinthians 13:1-13 ~

Cessationists view verse 8 where it says that prophecies shall fail, tongues shall cease, and knowledge shall vanish away as having occurred now. They believe that verse 10 has also occurred—the perfect has come in the Bible being completed and, therefore, we do not need the manifestation gifts of the Holy Spirit any more. This interpretation is incorrect. The Word of God is perfect, but the perfect that this verse is speaking of is none other than Jesus Christ our Lord; it is speaking of His second coming, for when He comes back in all the fullness of His Glory, we will then no longer need the manifestation of His Spirit among us for we will have Him in His fullness! It is now that we see dimly like through a mere glass, but when He comes in His fullness, in His return, we will then see Him face to face. Now we know in part, and we do still prophesy, although only in part, but when He returns we will know fully and our every question and wonder will be answered and understood, for we will be in the absolute fullness of His Presence. What we have now is but a glimpse of what is to come. His Spirit among us even when strongly felt and demonstrated is but a taste of what is to come. Now we are mere children learning to move and function in His grace and anointing. Faith, hope, and love, however, will abide forever in eternity with Him.

Lost and Found

It is understandable how this cessationist viewpoint came to be. After all, for many years during the Dark Ages and the years to follow, the manifestation gifts of the Holy Spirit did, for the most part, dry up as the Church struggled to shine forth. It was during this time that the gifts and manifestation of the Holy Spirit were rather "lost." I think of this time in history as being somewhat similar to the quiet years between the Old and New Testaments, similar in this regard: His people were not hearing from Him on a large scale and His revelation and inspiration was not being openly received. When I say revelation, let me clarify, I do not mean there is any new revelation outside of the Holy Scriptures. They are complete and cannot be added to; however, people during the Dark Ages were not receiving illumination of the Scriptures to much degree; all of this led to the Church being in a darkened state. That is why it was called the Dark Ages—things were dark. The Word of God, that brings light, was not readily available for the average Christian to read, and the Church services were spoken in the language of Latin, which the average person did not speak or understand. To make matters worse, corrupt teachings were being taught in the church such as *indulgences*—the teaching that people could buy their deceased loved one's way into Heaven by giving money to the church. Though there was a remnant of saints that moved in and experienced the manifestation gifts of the Spirit of God, they were often times shut down or excommunicated from the Church out of jealousy or disbelief. Some were even put to death. So for the most part, the manifest gifts of the Holy Spirit did cease for a time. It is not strange then that people would accept this carnal and natural state as the norm and try to explain it with Scripture.

Through a series of movements, God re-established the lost truths found in His Word regarding spiritual gifts. It was not until the Protestant Reformation of Martin Luther that the church began to come out of its darkened state. Revelation or illumination came to Martin Luther as he was reading the Scriptures. He, being a servant of God in the current church, saw the light of the Gospel. He saw with eyes of faith granted by God that the just shall live by faith. Martin Luther received the truth that is found in Ephesians 2:8-9, "For by grace you have been saved through faith, and that not of yourselves; it is the gift of God, not of works, lest anyone should boast." The foundational truth was restored with the Protestant Reformation that the "just shall live by faith" (see Habakkuk 2:4; Hebrews 10:38). It is only by exercising faith in the Son of God, Jesus Christ our Savior, that we can be saved. This was the first truth restored back to the church. Later, through a series of restorational movements, other lost truths found in the Scriptures were restored to the church.

During the 1800's, the Holiness Movement restored faith in God's sanctification (holy living and a set-apart life for God) and for divine healing. It was then that the truth about healing was rediscovered: "Is anyone among you sick? Let him call for the elders of the church, and let them pray over him, anointing him with oil in the name of the Lord" (James 5:14). The office of the Evangelist was re-established during this time. Circuit preachers who traveled on horseback ministered in tent meetings. Miracles and healings were seen in their ministry.

During the early 1900's, God brought forth the Pentecostal Movement. It was during this movement that the gift of tongues was re-established, along with the interpretation of tongues (see 1 Cor. 12:7-11). During the 1960's, the Charismatic Movement came into being. It is during this movement that God brought forth revelation of the Scriptures to produce faith for the charismatic gifts, or manifestation gifts, found in the twelfth chapter of 1 Corinthians. It was during this outpouring that believers began to move in prophecy, faith, healings, words of knowledge, words of wisdom, and discerning of spirits. Miracles began to be seen again in larger volumes in the church. The gifts and manifestation of the Holy Spirit were being re-discovered.

During the 1970's the Faith Movement was established. It was during this movement that the truth of receiving from God by faith in God and His written Word was emphasized. The office of the Teacher was established during this movement. The Teacher taught the believer to have faith in God's Word.

During the 1980's, the Prophetic Movement was established. During this movement, there was a re-emphasis on the prophetic, and the Lord re-established the office of the Prophet as well. The Prophet imparts and activates spiritual gifts within the church and brings forth the voice of God to reveal His heart regarding the building of His church.

During the 1990's, the Apostolic Movement was launched. This movement brought forth the office of the Apostle, or sent one, once again. This office was recognized as one who is sent to build and establish new works. Miracles are also part of the equipment of the Apostle.

The Saints Movement was birthed during the early 2000's. This movement does not emphasize any of the five-fold ministers, since they have already been established. With the establishment of the five-fold ministers, the believers or saints have been equipped for each of the offices (Apostle, Prophet, Evangelist, Pastor, and Teacher), carrying with them an anointing in that area, which they release and impart to the saints. "And He Himself gave some to be apostles, some prophets, some evangelists, and some pastors and teachers, for the equipping of the saints for the work of ministry, for the edifying of the body of Christ, till we all come to the unity of the faith and of the knowledge of the Son of God, to a perfect man, to the measure of the stature of the fullness of Christ;" (Ephesians 4:11-13). It is the saints, the believers, who are to be equipped with the anointing to do the work of the ministry in their sphere of influence. No longer is it a "one-man show." It is the saints, the body of Christ, who are to be the hands and feet of the Lord and His voice by echoing His Word from Heaven—pointing the way to Him and giving Him the glory! We, the saints, are to stretch forth our faith, believing for miracles to be released through us.[2]

We were lost, but now we are found because we put our faith in Jesus Christ, our Lord. The gifts and manifestations of the Spirit were lost, but now are found because God has restored them to His people and is restoring them to His people. As we seek, we find. He so wants to use us. Have there been misuses and abuses in the past? Yes, sure there have been. Every movement brings with it a mixture. Since fallen mankind is involved, imperfections are present. Nevertheless, God uses us and desires us to stretch forth our

---

2 For more reading on the movements of God see Dr. Bill Hamon's books: *The Eternal Church; The Day of the Saints; Prophetic Scriptures Yet To Be Fulfilled, and other books.* (Christian International, Santa Rosa Beach, FL)

faith and believe for Him to back up His Word with signs following—miracles included.

The Progression

There is a progression: first we believe in miracles, then we believe for a miracle, then we receive our miracle, then we believe to be used in miracles, then we experience a miracle, then we walk in miracles.

Before any of it happens, generally, we must believe for it. Unless someone else's faith was used to do the believing and bring forth the miracle, we must believe. Faith precedes miracles. That's why faith is listed among the power gifts of the Holy Spirit (faith, healing, and miracles). Without faith there can be no miracles. Faith is the arm that reaches into Heaven to receive the miraculous from God. Faith also is what enables us to move out and pray for the sick and hurting and believe for God to do a miracle through us. First and foremost, we must believe.

Before the woman with the issue of blood received her miracle of healing, she believed. She said, "If only I may touch His clothes, I shall be made well." She touched Him and was healed (Mark 5:28). In the region of Gennesaret, the people also believed, and as many as reached out and touched the hem of His garment were healed (see Mark 6:56). While in Capernaum, a centurion came and pleaded with the Lord to heal his servant that was at home paralyzed and tormented. Jesus replied that he would come and heal him. Jesus was then surprised at the centurion's great faith, for the centurion said that he was not worthy for Him to come to his home, but to just say the word and his servant would be healed. The centurion then explained that he understood authority because he was a man under authority and had servants whom he was over and who did as he commanded, so Jesus could, in similar manner, exercise His authority and heal his servant by simply speaking the word. Jesus applauded this centurion's great faith by saying he had not seen such faith in all of Israel! He spoke the word, and his servant was healed (see Matthew 8:5-13).

By contrast, the people in Nazareth, His hometown, did not believe. They said, "Is this not the carpenter, the Son of Mary...?" (Mark 6:3). They allowed familiarity to hamper them from believing. As a result, the Word says that Jesus could do no mighty works there. He only could lay His hands on a few sick people and heal them (see Mark 6:4-6). Jesus went without honor there in His hometown, and it cost the people their miracles. Jesus was astonished at their lack of faith. Believing is a key to receiving from God.

"So then faith comes by hearing and hearing by the word of God" (Romans 10:17). As we hear the Scriptures about Jesus performing miracles, and we hear the Word of God preached concerning God's miraculous power, faith wells up within our soul and buds forth to God. Faith is both a gift and a fruit. As faith flowers, it smiles up at God. He gently reaches down and touches this new blossom with the tip of His fingers and smiles back as He tenderly admires its growth of expectation. Faith makes God smile back! We are but faithful flowers in

God's garden of grace. He tends His garden and cares for His growing blossoms.

Jesus' disciples grew in faith as they watched Him reach out to those He daily came in contact with. Their faith grew as they watched Him respond to the hungry hearts of expectation around Him. And they began to understand His heart more and more. Miracle after miracle, they watched and learned. There was the deliverance of the man with the legion of unclean spirits. Jesus took authority over them and commanded them to leave the man, bringing deliverance to this previously tortured soul. Then, there was the healing of the woman with the issue of blood, which she had for twelve years! Some were selected by Jesus to accompany Him in the raising of Jairus' daughter from the dead. With each miracle, His disciples began to understand a little bit more. And they believed (see Mark 5:1-43).

The disciples also had received *their* miracles; they had freely received, and now it was time for them to give freely. Peter had watched as his mother-in-law received her miracle. While their faith may have been rocked a bit while riding the waves of trial on the Sea of Galilee, they had all watched in wonder as Jesus stilled the sea with His Word. And after fishing all day and catching nothing, Peter obeyed Jesus' instructions to "cast the net on the other side" and, as a result, he received a heap of fish! In all of this training, they received their miracles! Now, as His disciples, who had been in training, it was time for them to be sent out as apostles to practice what they had learned and to be His hands and feet, to preach the Kingdom of God and to walk in miracles. So, after they had watched and learned, the day arrived for them to do as He did. Jesus sent out His disciples giving them authority to go in His Name and to do His work. Like an employer who empowers His employees, Jesus empowered them to go and do His great exploits. They were spiritual deputies, armed with His grace and power. Then Jesus backed them up by releasing His miraculous power through them. They became his expanded body. (See Mark 1:29-31; 3:13-19; 4:35-41; Luke 5:1-11; Matthew 10:8; and Mark 6:7,12-13.)

After getting their "feet wet", the new apostles returned and told Jesus all they said and did on their adventure. However, their learning continued as they watched and even participated in the giving out of the loaves and fish. As Jesus blessed this small lunch, He miraculously increased it to feed the 5000! Later, Jesus repeated the same miracle and fed 4000 more. Each time the disciples were used to assist Jesus in handing out the lunches, and in doing so, they participated in the miracle! They saw the compassion that selflessly motivated Jesus with each miracle, and they began to understand more and more the heart of their Master. Little children were brought to Jesus and the disciples tried to shove them off, but Jesus cared for the little ones; He corrected His disciples for their actions and gathered the children to Himself. He cared about blind Bartimaeus, even though the disciples tried to brush him aside as insignificant; Jesus *cared*, and He reached out in compassion and healed this blind beggar, who cried out in faith (see Mark 10:46-52). His disciples stood amazed and they longed to be like Him—in heart.

Jesus is all about multiplication. That's partially why we were made in the image of God; He wanted to reproduce after His own kind—children made in His image. So, after sending out the twelve, the time came for increase. He now sends out the seventy others whom He had appointed (see Luke 10:1). The seventy returned with joy, for they had great success in their ministry. Jesus was equally, if not more, joyful than they were, for the Scripture tells us that He leaped for joy! Jesus remarked that He saw Satan falling like lightening from the Heavens as a result of their ministry! This absolutely thrilled Him, for His disciples were "getting it." It is the joy of any true teacher to see their students understand and apply their lessons. Jesus declared, "Behold, I give you the authority to trample on serpents and scorpions, and over all the power of the enemy, and nothing shall by any means hurt you" (Luke 10:19). Then Jesus thanked the Father for hiding such things from the wise but revealing them to babes. The word translated "rejoiced", to describe Jesus' demeanor while proclaiming this, is the Greek word *"agalliaō"*, which according to *Strong's Exhaustive Concordance* means to "jump for joy"! Jesus is still literally thrilled when His disciples "get it." He does remind His disciples, though, not to rejoice in the fact that the demons are subject to us in His Name, but that our names are recorded in Heaven. After His death and resurrection, the day approached for Jesus to return to His Father in Heaven. Before ascending, however, He left a great commission to be

In His Presence

embraced by His disciples (past, present and future), to go into the entire world and to preach the Gospel, *with signs following* (see Mark 16:15-18). Jesus continues to back up His Word and His delegated authority with His miraculous power.

The First Miracle

You may say, "Oh, but I could never operate in such a manifestation of the Spirit. Who am I?" The truth is, if you have Christ as your Savior and you have been baptized with the Holy Spirit, you have what it takes to go out and begin to minister to people as His Spirit leads you. You simply learn just as the first disciples learned, by spending time with Him. As they spent time with Jesus, they learned His ways and heart. And as Jesus spent time with His Father in prayer, so we are to spend time with Him in prayer and in His Word. Jesus is with us by His Spirit, and He is the one who is ministering through us.

To move in miracles, there must be a first miracle. Even Jesus had a first miracle. It was during the wedding feast at Cana. It was during this celebration, that the wine had run out. Mary, the mother of Jesus, brought the problem to her Son's attention. He responded that His time had not yet come, meaning that He gets His directives from His Heavenly Father. Up to this point, Jesus had done no miracles. The Scriptures tell us that this was the beginning of the signs (or wonders, or miracles) that Jesus was to manifest. Jesus had the servants fill the water jars with water to the brim. Then the miracle occurred: He changed the water into wine. This new

151

wine was of the finest quality. They were all amazed that the best wine was kept for last, as that was not the usual custom. Jesus was invited to the wedding; He was in attendance; His Presence was there. Where His Presence is ... miracles happen! Beloved, He is in you; He is in attendance; His Presence goes with you (see John 2:1-12)!

You may say, "Oh, but *my* time has not yet come." In saying or thinking that, you are most likely merely feeling a fear of man, a fear of making a mistake, or a feeling of inferiority that would cause you to draw back. "But we are not of those who draw back to perdition, but of those who believe to the saving of the soul" (Hebrews 10:39). The time is *now* for miracles, "For indeed, the kingdom of God is within you" (Luke 17:21).

It has nothing to do with how *we feel*, because it really has nothing to do with *us*. I remember the first time the Lord used me to bring a miracle of healing to an individual. It was at my church and I was doing altar ministry. I often times pray for the sick, as the Scriptures tell us to. This particular morning, a woman came to the altar believing for healing. (I honestly cannot recall the details of her distress.) I remember thinking that she should go to another lady in the church that was well known for moving in manifestations of healing. This woman wanted *me* to pray for her though. To make matters worse, *I* was not feeling well physically either, and I remember feeling inadequate and wishing I could just go home. Nevertheless, I prayed for her. It wasn't an earthshaking prayer; I felt no goose bumps. I am not sure what she felt. She left the altar seemingly unaffected. However, after I returned home, I received a phone call from the woman. She was very excited and wanted to tell me that her symptoms had completely disappeared! She was healed! To God be all the glory! So, you see, it has nothing at all to do with us! It is all about Him. Such healings and miracles are for His glory. They are like road signs pointing the way to Him.

We must catch His heart for the hurting people around us. As we do, we will feel the same compassion that He felt when He gave sight to the blind, and healed the sick, and fed the multitudes. His compassion must be our motivation. And it is selfless.

You may ask as His disciples did in John 6:28, "What shall we do, that we may work the works of God?" That is a good question and one that does not go unanswered; Jesus answers it for us, "This is the work of God, that you believe in Him whom He sent" (John 6:29). Do you want to do the works of God? Only believe! Believe on the One who lives inside you. It is by His Spirit that His works are wrought. Be His hands, be His feet, and be His mouthpiece. His Presence is with you.

Mary, the mother of Jesus, had some additional advice for His servants. She said to them,

"Whatever He says to you, do it" (John 2:5). As we, His modern-day servants, are obedient to His indwelling Spirit, and step out believing in Him, doing what He says to do, we become His functioning Body here on earth and His will is done. For all things are possible to him who believes and follows His Word. My friends, miracles are found *in His Presence*.

Prayer

Dear Jesus, I dare to ask You to use me in miracles. Use me to pray for the sick and see them recover. Use me to reach out in your Name and as I do, deliver your people from the oppression and influences of the dark one. May your light shine through me to bring miracles of salvation, healing, and deliverance. Help me to have Your heart of compassion for the lost and hurting, and to be obedient to Your promptings, even when I don't feel like it. The results are in Your hand, oh Lord. And in all of this, may You be glorified. I desire to move in Your powerful Presence. Amen.

CHAPTER 10

The Protection of His Presence

He who dwells in the secret place of the Most
High shall abide under the shadow of the
Almighty. I will say of the LORD, "He is my
refuge and my fortress; My God, in Him I
will trust."

~ PSALM 91:1-2 ~

WHERE DO YOU go when you're afraid? Where do you run to?
When I was a child, I remember hiding under the blankets
when I was afraid at night. If I saw a shadow or heard a noise,
quickly I would pull the blankets up over my head to protect
me from the would-be monsters. As adults, we find new shelters to hide in. For some, it is drugs and alcohol. For others,
it is relationships on which we have grown dependent. Some
hide by burying themselves in their work; they get lost among
the clutter of the busyness of life. Still others hide by with-
drawing into the solitude of their four walls ... depressed and
alone.

The Almighty longs to be our refuge and our fortress. When we *abide* in Him, we also abide *under* His almighty shadow. He longs to gather us up under His wing of protection. The question is: Are we willing to come under His wing? When Jesus walked the earth, he grieved over Jerusalem as He observed their unwillingness to come unto Him: "O Jerusalem, Jerusalem, the one who kills the prophets and stones those who are sent to her! How often I wanted to gather your children together, as a hen gathers her brood under her wings, but you were not willing" (Luke 13:34)! Jesus longed for them, and He longs for us. He desires to gather us up ... to gather *you* up ... and shelter you under His wing, close to His heart, where you are near Him and protected. As we respond by running beneath the shelter of His wing, He *covers* us. Having the Almighty God for a covering is the ultimate protection. His Presence overshadows us and shelters us through our life's journey and trials.

When something is "covered," it is protected because it is hidden from sight. The enemy does not see it, so he does not go after it. That is how it is in God, we are hidden in Him and His protection keeps us out of the sight of the enemy. In the book *The Hiding Place*, Corey Ten Boom wrote about how she hid the Jews from the Nazi's during WWII, in a secret room—behind a false wall. There in a small room, the size of a closet, God's people hid from the enemy. However, their real protection was in God. He was their protection and their hiding place. Psalm 32:7 says, "You are my hiding place; You shall preserve me from trouble; You shall surround me with songs of deliverance." His Presence is our protection, like the old hymn, "Rock of Ages" says, "Rock of ages, cleft for me. Let me hide thyself in Thee."

We too can pray "prayers of protection" by asking the Lord to cover us, to protect us, and to hide us from the enemy. Usually, hiding has to do with fear. We hide because we are afraid. When the enemy pursues, we hide out of fear and we pray out of fear. However, it need not be that way. When the enemy of our souls pursues us, we can call out to God in *faith* that He will hear us and respond by hiding us from the enemy. The Word of God tells us: "By faith Moses, when he was born, was hidden three months by his parents, because they saw he was a beautiful child; and *they were not afraid* of the king's command" (Hebrews 11:23, emphasis mine). They hid him out of faith. Corrie Ten Boom hid the Jews out of faith. We too can exercise faith to believe God for protection—for Him to hide us from the enemy. When we do so, our faith becomes a shield; that's why the Bible calls it our "shield of faith" (see Ephesians 6:16). Even if fiery darts are thrown our way, with our shield of faith in place, they will bounce right off us. That's why His Word says, "... His truth shall be your shield and buckler. You shall not be afraid of the terror by night, nor of the arrow that flies by day," (Psalm 91:4-5).

God's protection is like great wings that shield us. His feathers cover us, the Bible tells us, as we hide beneath them. He soars above us like a great eagle, and we are like His young ones who fly beneath His protection and guidance as He raises us up and launches us out (see Exodus 19:4;

Deuteronomy 32:11; and Isaiah 40:31). There we are under the shelter of His wing. We soar under His covering, hidden in His shadow.

Flying Under Radar

Being hidden also safely positions us for our offensive missions for the Lord. Some family members of mine work in a plant where they make parts for one of our modern world's greatest inventions—the stealth bomber. This aircraft has the ability to perform its military objective and take out the enemy without being detected. Thus it is "hidden." God hides us in this fashion as well. He may give us a mission to do for His Kingdom, and He will protect us from the enemy in a "stealth" fashion as we carry it out. We are camouflaged from the enemy's sight as we "fly under the radar." In this way God protects us from being attacked or counterattacked from the forces of evil. Whenever I am about my Father's business in the Kingdom, I pray and ask Him to keep me under His almighty wing and protect me from the sight of the enemy.

We also can pray these prayers of protection for each other to protect us from the enemy's backlash. Whether we are missionaries in foreign lands or witnessing for Christ in our work place, we all need to be hidden in the Presence of the Lord and fly under the enemy's radar. It is there with Him that we are safe indeed. There is protection in His Presence.

Trust = Confidence

When we put our trust in Him for protection, it exercises our faith. We have our faith and trust in the Almighty God and therefore, we do not fear. Knowing that God is watching out for us produces a God-confidence. This confidence affects everything we do. When we know we are on God's mission and under His protection, we have a confidence that we walk in. This confidence is evident to those around us. It is a "blessed assurance." Because we have confidence in God's protection, we have faith to go wherever He is sending us and to do whatever He tells us to do, for He goes before us and is our rear guard. The only time we should be afraid is when we are going where He did not send us. When we are in God's will, His Presence is with us. Moses said to the Lord, "If Your Presence does not go with us, do not bring us up from here" (Exodus 33:15). Likewise, we don't dare pursue anything that we don't believe is God's will for us. For if there is safety and protection in God's Presence, then the opposite is also true: when we find ourselves outside of His Divine protection of His Presence, there is no safety. It is like walking in a storm with no umbrella.

The Umbrella in the Storm

When walking with your loved one under an umbrella, you are safe from the storm as long as you stay together under the umbrella, but the minute you depart from your loved one and step out from under an umbrella that they are holding, you get soaked! So it is with God. As long as we walk with Him, He holds up an umbrella for us and keeps us protected from the hard-pressed rain, but the moment we depart from walking in His way, we step out from under His protective covering of grace; we are now out on our own—without a covering.

Walking with God under His umbrella of protection is what enables us to endure the hardship of the rain. You may ask, "But why does there have to be a rain storm? Why, I have even been hit by some hailstones!" Rain is necessary to make things grow here on the earth. The rain of adversity likewise, is the ground that faith is grown in. It is when the weather is less than perfect and storms persist, sometimes hitting us sideways, that we realize how much we need Him. There, under the covering of His Presence, He draws us near Him and shelters us from the storm.

The Horse and the Mule

Do not be like the horse or like the mule,
which have no understanding,
which must be harnessed with bit and bridle,
else they will not come near you.

~ PSALM 32:9 ~

When we get self-confident, we venture out where we should not. We may get ahead of God because we think we know where we are going and assume that He is right behind us.

Moses wanted God to go *before him*, not be behind him! The Scripture does tell us that God is our *also* our rear-guard, but that is only when He *first* goes before us. "For the LORD will go before you, and the God of Israel will be your rear guard" (Isaiah 52:12). We want God going before us, to be with us, and behind us; that is when we are under His circular umbrella of protection.

Sometimes I go horseback riding with my good friend, MaryJane. We trail ride through the wooded and fielded areas around her home. There are times when we have to hold the horses back because they want to take off running. We are the same way with the Lord. Sometimes we get excited and want to run ahead of Him. This is usually because we think we know where we are going and can't wait to get there. It is then that God has to keep His hand upon us and rein us in a bit. If we get out ahead of Him, we are out of God's timing and there can be danger on the horizon. Perhaps the road is not yet prepared for us to travel on. If that is the case, there will be rocks, craters, and boulders in our way. The ground could not be solid and could slip out from under our feet causing us to fall.

On occasion, the Israelites found themselves out from under God's protection, and it was always when they thought they knew the way better and doubted in God's ways. For example, King Saul got ahead of God when he grew tired and impatient waiting for Samuel to come and make an offering unto the Lord at Gilgal. After seven days, the people began to scatter from Saul, so out of fear and impatience, he went ahead and made an offering unto the

Lord. In doing so, Saul disobeyed Prophet Samuel's previous, explicit instructions to wait for his return in seven days. It was Samuel's, not Saul's position to offer unto and entreat the Lord. When Prophet Samuel returned, he expressed the Lord's displeasure in Saul's presumptuous actions (see 1 Samuel 10:8; 13:1-14).

Another time King Saul disobeyed the Lord and instead followed his own selfish desires was when he allowed the people to take some spoils after a battle that he was explicitly told by God not to take. When Prophet Samuel confronted him about it, he made the lame excuse that it was taken to offer up to the Lord. Thus, the well-known Biblical expression was born: "To obey is better than sacrifice" (see 1 Samuel 15:1-23). Saul walked in disobedience to the Lord's commands and, therefore, he walked out from God's will. When we are out from under God's will, we are out from under His protection, and we are out from under His blessings as well, for we are not walking in obedience to His directives. For these acts of disobedience, for running ahead like a wild, unbroken horse, King Saul lost his throne.

Other times we get out from under God's protective umbrella of His Presence by lagging behind like a stubborn mule. When the twelve leaders were sent into the Promise Land to spy it out, only two of them came back to the people with a good report of faith in God (Joshua and Caleb). Ten of the spies doubted that God would take care of them in the Promised Land. In this case, they allowed fear, doubt, and unbelief to keep them from stepping into the place that God had for them. They feared the giants of the land. Joshua and Caleb, the Bible tells us, had a different spirit from the other ten spies. They had a spirit of faith to believe God for His promises. After hearing the disbelief of the others, the Bible says,

> But Joshua the son of Nun and Caleb the son of Jephunneh, who were among those who had spied out the land, tore their clothes; and they spoke to all the congregation of the children of Israel, saying: "The land we passed through to spy out is an exceedingly good land. If the LORD delights in us, then He will bring us into this land and give it to us, 'a land which flows with milk and honey.' Only do not rebel against the LORD, nor fear the people of the land, for they are our bread; *their protection has departed from them*, and the LORD is with us. Do not fear them"

Numbers 14:6-9 (emphasis mine).

Joshua and Caleb recognized that the enemy had lost *their* protection and that the Presence of the Lord was with them. Protection was now with the Israelites *because the Presence of the Lord was with them*—He covered them. Unfortunately, the others did not mix this Word with faith, and so they could not enter into what God had for them because of unbelief. Friends, we must have faith in where God is leading us and walk in the warmth and safety of His Presence. It is then that we have His protection.

Sanctuary

A sanctuary is commonly known as the inner place of a church. We hold our church services in the sanctuary. In Old Testament times, God gave instruction for the building of the tabernacle and later the temple. Both of these structures had an inner sanctuary, which was where God's Presence was to dwell.

The word sanctuary also means: a shelter, safe place, or refuge. The reason for this is people would go to the sanctuary to find shelter and safety in times of trouble. When I think of the word sanctuary, I can't help but think of the fictional story *The Hunchback of Notre-Dame* by Victor Hugo. As the story goes, this poor deformed hunchback of a man, Quasimodo, falls in love with the beautiful Esmeralda and rescues her from a sure death, after she was falsely accused of murder. Quasimodo dramatically carries Esmeralda to the cathedral of Notre-Dame while declaring, "Sanctuary!" There he kept her safe within the bell-tower of the cathedral, where he too found sanctuary.

The early church would extend sanctuary or asylum to those seeking protection from false accusation. Rules were put in place to govern this practice. Political asylum likewise is granted by some countries for the accused, who are deemed worthy to seek shelter from attack until they can stand trial; this also can be termed as "sanctuary." So, the word "sanctuary" has come to mean, in a broad sense, a place of safety. But who is it that is really our protector? It is the Lord Almighty! A true sanctuary is such only because of His Presence within, as demonstrated in this verse, where the Lord God says, "And let them make Me a sanctuary, that I may dwell among them" (Exodus 25:8). The whole purpose for the original sanctuary being built was for God's Presence to be among us. Today, we gather in our church sanctuaries to seek His Presence and worship Him, leaving the hustle and bustle of the world outside the doors. While within the inner sanctuary, we focus on Him and call upon His Name. He meets with us and makes His Presence known, and as He does, we know that we are safe in His Presence. *He is our sanctuary.*

While it is true that He is our sanctuary, we also are His, in this sense ... we are the temple or sanctuary of the Most High God, as this Scripture tells us: "Or do you not know that your body is the temple of the Holy Spirit who is in you, whom you have from God, and you are not your own?" (1 Corinthians 6:19). Another word for temple is sanctuary. So, while it is true that He is our sanctuary, we are also His sanctuary. As Christians, God's very Spirit takes up residence within us. Therefore, not only do we *have* sanctuary, we *are* a sanctuary. Because we are a sanctuary, we should feel and carry God's Presence and peace with us, being aware of His Presence and the safety He brings and, therefore, making others feel safe as well. When we come into contact with others who are distraught, we can offer them the "sanctuary" of His Presence.

The name of the LORD is a strong tower;
the righteous run to it and are safe.

~ Proverbs 18:10 ~

When we call upon His Name, He answers us—He shows up! Because of our right standing with Him we run to Him in times of trouble, and He lifts us up and protects us with His powerful Presence. There is no place I would rather be than in His Presence. He is our strong tower—our fortress. In a world filled with fearful news reports, terrorist threats, identity theft, and persecutions, we must have faith in Him—our strong tower—and take comfort in the protection of His Presence.

Prayer

Lord Jesus, You are my hiding place. I put my trust in You. I hide myself in You. Remind me throughout my day that You are there waiting for me, covering me, and protecting me. I put my trust in You and You alone. I run to you and am safe. Thank you for being my protection in times of trouble and for covering me as I move out under Your directions. Amen.

CHAPTER 11

§

Pursued by His Presence

For the Son of Man has come to seek and to
save that which was lost.

~ LUKE 19:10 ~

WE ALL HAVE times when we feel lost; even after calling upon
Jesus, our Good Shepherd, and coming into His sheep-fold,
we still occasionally find ourselves unwittingly temporarily
"lost" (although we really are not lost in the sense of losing
our salvation). We are momentarily lost amongst the clutter of life, buried beneath our mounds of troubles, and lured
away by the glitter of life's fool's gold. We become overwhelmed with life's circumstances and temporarily lose our
bearings. It is like our spiritual GPS has lost its signal and we
can't find our way.

Kathy Wypij

The Pursuit of the Lost Sheep

In the parable of the lost sheep (see Luke 15:4-7), Jesus tells of a shepherd who leaves the ninety-nine sheep to go and seek the one who wandered away and became lost. Many years ago, my husband and I raised sheep. We had a flock of over thirty-five at one time and had close to 100 lambs born in a year's time! Sometimes the sheep would wander off. Even though we kept a nice big pasture for them to graze in, they would think the grass was greener on the other side of the fence and would look for a way to get under the fence to wander off. Then we would hear a knock on our front door. When we answered the door we would find someone standing there telling us that our sheep were in the road, and they stopped their car to tell us. We would then thank them and apologize for the inconvenience. Then, like good shepherds, we would go to collect our wanderers. Like wandering sheep, we too get carried away from time to time with the things of this world and our pursuit of them. Climbing the corporate ladder, accomplishing our goals, providing for our families, all can become pursuits that lead us further and further away from the flock and our Good Shepherd. Sometimes we reach for just one bite of that "greener grass" and, before you know it, we are on the other side of the hill and spiritually far, far away.

Jesus is a much better shepherd than any of us could possibly be. He is well aware of all our wanderings. There is no place we can wander off to that is out of His sight. Even when we go out beyond where we should be, He keeps an eye on us. Therefore, as His sheep, we are never really lost.

In the parable of the lost sheep, Jesus tells us that the shepherd leaves the ninety-nine to seek out the one who became lost. In doing so, He demonstrates that each of us matters so much to Him. When we had our little farm, we sometimes had to "count our losses" when things didn't go well. However, Jesus, our Great Shepherd, never "counts His losses" in the sense of giving up on those who are lost, but He does "count His losses" in the sense that He takes count of those who are lost or wandered off, and he seeks them out. Why? He does so because He cares. Everyone is important to Him. None can be counted off as a "loss." All must be pursued. He pursues us because He cares for us. He searches for us until we are found.

When we are out where we shouldn't be—busy chasing greener grass—we are vulnerable to the wolves that desire to devour us. The boundaries Christ gives us, as the Great Shepherd of our souls, are there for our protection. The commandments found in His Word and the directions He gives us in prayer are in fact our fence-line. Staying near the Shepherd of our souls is where we need to be, and it is there that we are safe. When we wander off to places that He is not leading us, we get ourselves into trouble.

When Mike and I raised sheep we found that the way to get sheep to come home was to call out to them and shake the grain bucket. The sheep would hear us calling them and would hear that grain bucket shaking the grain inside, and they would come a running. They knew that the goodness that was within that bucket was much richer food than all the green grass the world had to offer. They left their "greener grass" and came home for the food that their shepherds were offering them.

We are the sheep of His pasture. We hear His voice, the Bible tells us, and the voice of a stranger we will not follow (see John 10:4-5). His Word contains the rich food that fills our souls, and His Spirit speaks to ours as we give time to listen for His voice. He has buckets of revelation and anointing that He pours out upon us. He pursues us. Whether we are out there with a flock of others or out on our own, either way, He pursues us because He cares for us. You are worth going after. You are counted among His flock. When one is missing, He pursues, He seeks, and He saves. It is then that we find the peace and pleasure of His Presence and can echo the Psalmist's words: "The LORD is my shepherd; I shall not want. He makes me to lie down in green pastures; He leads me beside the still waters. He restores my soul..." (Psalm 23:1-3). Amen.

The Pursuit of the Lost Coin

Jesus went on speaking to His people in another parable. This time He used the metaphor of a woman who had some silver coins and lost one (see Luke 15:8-10). She didn't just chalk it up as lost. No, on the contrary, the loss of this coin was a great loss to her. This lost coin had great value; therefore, she lit a lamp and searched diligently for the coin. She swept the floor and searched and searched until she found it. Once the coin was found, she rejoiced and called her friends to rejoice with her. Jesus said in a similar way that all of Heaven rejoices over one sinner who turns to follow the Lord.

He is in pursuit of us daily. He wants us close to Him. He values us like a piece of silver. You have value to God. He cares for you. You count to Him. When He does a "head count" you are to be in that number. If you are not "present", if your heart has taken a turn, if your thoughts became captive by the world, then He is searching for you. He will leave no stone unturned until you are back in the palm of His hand again, all because you are so valuable to Him.

The Pursuit of the Lost Son

The parables continue only this time Jesus speaks of a father who had two sons (see Luke 15:11-32). The youngest son boldly asked his father to give him an early inheritance. His father consented even though it was a selfish and immature request that greatly dishonored his father. This young son then went on his merry way and spent all he was given on wild living. Then hard times fell upon this son and he found himself working at the lowly job of feeding pigs. He was so hungry that he even hungered after the pods that the pigs were eating. After sinking to this level—after coming to an end of himself—this young son finally had the light of dawn come to him. He remembered how his father was well off, had several men employed under him, and how well he lived while with his father. He had the idea of returning home to work for his father. He realized that he had not behaved well and, therefore, he did not feel worthy to be called his father's son any more but was willing to simply be counted among his father's hired hands.

This son turned around—he started down the road to return home. His father saw him coming down the road and held no grudge. Instead, his heart was filled with compassion for his son and was overjoyed at his return, so he ran down the road to meet him. This father hugged and kissed his son. He then called his servants to robe him, and honor him, and arrange for a party. The father exclaimed that his son was dead but now is alive again; he was lost but now is found!

This parable is a picture of our heavenly Father and His love for all of us. If we use our free-will to walk away from Him, He allows us to, but He longs for our return home. He watches for us to come back to Him. He is waiting for us to come to our senses and return to Him with gratitude for all He has done for us. Then He showers us with blessings! But the greatest blessing of all is the blessing of His Presence. Being with Him is the greatest blessing of all.

The older son lived with his father and never became lost. However, this older son, though living under his father's roof, never realized how valued he was for he felt jealous after the return of his younger brother. He accused his father of showing favoritism to his little brother, saying that his father never threw a party for him. His father then had to reassure the older son of his worth to him. He told him that all he had was his. We too, must remind ourselves that all God our Father has is ours. The Bible tells us that He withholds no good thing to those who love Him (see Psalms 84:11). He provides for us and cares for us. We must not lose sight of the fact that we are extremely valuable to Him.

Just as the shepherd went after the sheep, the woman searched for the lost coin, and the Father watched for the return of his lost son, so too, God longs for and pursues us to come unto Him. We are His. We belong to Him. We are his valued treasure. He searches for us like the lost coin—like a buried treasure—and awaits our return as the loving Father that He is, all because we are so very valuable to Him.

The Pursuit of the Buried Treasure

We have all either read books or seen movies about buried treasure. The thought of something of great value lying beneath the surface of the earth fascinates us. For archeologists, the pursuit of buried treasure becomes a reality as they dedicate their lives to the discovery of lost ruins and buried treasures. For most of us, however, the thought of discovering buried treasure remains a dream that for the most part is not experienced. Sometimes, however, we find something of great worth buried beneath the boxes of clutter in the attic or within the mounds of things hoarded by generations past out in the garage and when they are re-discovered, we are overjoyed because we have laid our hands upon a *lost treasure*.

I remember such a day when my brother, Mike, and I were busy settling our dad's estate. We were sorting out a bunch of hoarded junk in the basement when Mike found something special. He saw some small buckets of stone (the type that is used in ground cover for landscapers) and as he opened them, he felt strangely compelled to run his fingers through the small pebbles. When he did, something sparkled beneath the otherwise ordinary stones. It was silver! The whole bucket was full of silver coins! He had discovered a buried treasure right there in the basement of our late father! He was overjoyed as he called me on the phone, and we rejoiced together for our find! The treasure was divided up among our father's heirs.

In His Word, Jesus tells us a parable of a lost treasure that was buried in a field (see Matthew 13:44.) When a man came upon this buried treasure and found it, he was overjoyed! He then hid the treasure for Himself and went and sold all he had to purchase that field. He then possessed the whole field and all the treasure that was buried within it.

Jesus Himself is that man who gave all He had to buy back the lost world. You and I are that which was buried beneath the ruins of our own short history—you and I, who are held hostage by the soot of today's struggles and the decay of yesterday's problems. We have been unable to rise out of our surroundings. We needed Someone to dig us out—Someone to pull us out from our stuck situation—Someone to separate us from the hold of the world we live in. The dirt that surrounds us has become attached to our very being. But there is One who *sees* us; He is able to see beneath the film of worldly filth. He sees something sparkle out from the cracks of hardened clay. He sees our eternal worth—our destiny—our purpose—our innocence that is in need of repair yet present there beneath the garbage that was thrown upon us. He reaches down with His Almighty hand and takes a hold of us by His mighty grip of grace and pulls us up—out from the hold of the world and draws us unto Himself.

We are now free. Free from the decay that was working its way within us. Free from the rust of sin that was growing upon us and working its existence within the fiber of our being. Free from the maggots of evil that were eating away at our morals, hopes, and beliefs. We are free because we have been found by the Seeker of all seekers, the Pursuer of all pursuers, the Lover of our souls—Jesus Christ our Savior! He came to seek and save the lost. He is the Mighty Archeologist! We are His gems, His treasure, and His find. We were lost but now are found! And, we are forever His.

The Pursuit of the Priceless Pearl

Again, the kingdom of heaven is like a
merchant seeking beautiful pearls, who, when
he had found one pearl of great price, went
and sold all that he had and bought it.

~ MATTHEW 13:45-46 ~

Sometimes we struggle with our worth. We think we are of little value, that no one cares, and that our lives are virtually of no importance. This is far from the truth. Our lives are of great value to God. He has created you and me with a purpose in life.

Our lives are stories that are yet unfolding and, therefore, not fully told. The last chapters to our lives are not written yet, and we hold the pen. Tomorrow is a blank page on which a beautiful story can be written, and not just a story—not just fiction—but a true story that speaks to others out of a life of experience and of overcoming life's obstacles by applying principles of truth with God's guidance—a story that inspires others. 2 Corinthians 3:3 says, "Clearly you are an epistle of Christ, ministered by us, written not with ink but by the Spirit of the living God, not on tablets of stone but on tablets of flesh, that is, of the heart."

This life that is yet unfolding is like a precious pearl that is being developed throughout the hours and days of time. Pearls do not develop overnight, but are formed within an oyster over time. The making of a pearl is a unique process; it is actually the turning of an irritating circumstance into something wonderful. When an oyster's shell is invaded by an irritant, the oyster allows that irritant to be worked over into its very character. It is rolled over again and again within the fiber of its being. The pearl then begins to take shape, slowly building upon itself until finally the end result occurs—a beautiful and costly pearl. These pearls are greatly sought after because of their great worth. They are then fashioned into jewelry in the same way as precious gemstones.

Your life is a precious pearl in the making. When life throws irritations your way, choose to allow them to work on your character. Allow them to mold and shape within your being. Allow the Spirit of the Lord to use them to bring patience, goodness, and self-control into your life. Allow them to shape your life into the pearl that you were created to be. You are the pearl of great cost. The Merchant is the Lord who gave up all the glory of heaven to come to earth for you. You were bought with the price of His precious blood. You are His precious pearl of great price.

When we are captured by the realization of His great love for us, and the great value that He places upon us, and how He gave up everything for us, we are so filled with love and appreciation that we then see Him as *our* Pearl of great cost. Now we desire to sell all for Him—our priceless Pearl.

The Pursuit of the Pursued

When we realize the great love He has for us, that He left the comforts and glory of heaven to come to earth in the passionate pursuit of our soul, that He laid down His very life in exchange for our freedom, that our life was so valuable to Him that He traded all to purchase us, how can we not lay down our lives in return? This is where this great love is reciprocated. "We love because He first loved us" (1 John 4:19). His love, when realized and experienced, moves us to love Him in return. This great love changes our viewpoint in life and rearranges our priorities. Now, because of His great love for us, we have a glimpse of the Kingdom of Heaven and desire yet more of Him. He sought after us; He searched us out and called us out of the darkness. He left the ninety-nine and came after us. He swept the house clean in search of us. He left no stone unturned in His all-out pursuit of us. He waited patiently for us when we were out sowing our wild oats. He drew us out of the miry clay, cleaned us up, and called us back to our purpose for living.

He confirmed to us our great value to Him and called us His precious ones, His pearls, His gems. Then, He placed us, His solitaire diamond, in the midst of other precious gems—like a family, so we are no longer alone (see Psalm 68:6).

All of this—all of His loving pursuit of us—causes us to but taste of the things to come. We but only catch a glimpse of Him because He is so infinite. Our hearts are now ignited to burn passionately for Him. Now, like a love-struck lover, *we pursue Him.* Our souls long for Him. Our hearts identify with the words of the Psalmist when he said: "O God, You are my God; early will I seek You; my soul thirsts for You; my flesh longs for You in a dry and thirsty land where there is no water" (Psalm 63:1).

Prayer

Lord Jesus, You sought me and bought me with Your own precious blood. You pursued me and pursue me. You watch my every step. You know my every thought. You care about me. After all You have done for me, I can only give You my heart in return. You are my precious Pearl, my Treasure. I long for You and You alone. In all my seeking, may I find You more and more. Amen.

Let us know, Let us *pursue* the knowledge of
the LORD. His going forth is established as
the morning; He will come to us like the rain,
like the latter and former rain to the earth.

~ HOSEA 6:3 (emphasis mine) ~

CHAPTER 12

§

Consumed by His Presence

For the LORD your God is a consuming fire, a
jealous God.

~ DEUTERONOMY 4:24 ~

WHEN I WAS a child, my parents owned a small business comprised of a store and restaurant. Behind the building was a hillside that consisted of grass and trees. On one sunshiny day, I recall standing in the kitchen of the restaurant and watching out the back window. While I was watching, two of the neighborhood boys came into view; they squatted down on the ground and pulled out some hot dogs and matches. They struck a match and held it to the dry grass that covered the ground. Apparently, they were on an adventure to have an innocent hot dog roast. Much to their surprise, the grass took off in flames! The boys fled as the hillside turned ablaze. I scrambled off, too, in search of my father to announce the FIRE! Short story is the fire was put out on the hill, but the boys were caught and the seat of their pants set ablaze with the wrath of their parent's chastening!

Because the hillside was dry and brittle it easily caught fire, and the area where the fire burned was consumed. Sin also is dry and lifeless. A sinful life is a dead life. Scripture tells us that God's fiery Presence burns against His enemies. This results in their consumption. For example, Isaiah 1:28 says, "The destruction of transgressors and of sinners shall be together, and those who forsake the LORD shall be consumed." Another example is 2 Kings 1:12 which says, "So Elijah answered and said to them, 'If I am a man of God, let fire come down from heaven and consume you and your fifty men.' And the fire of God came down from heaven and consumed him and his fifty."

Our Lord God is a consuming fire. That is a fire that burns up everything it comes in contact with. As was stated in a previous chapter, God is a Holy God and, therefore, sin cannot dwell in His Presence. Like a struck match to wood, hay, and stubble, so is the fire of God's Presence to the chaff of wickedness. Over and over again the Old Testament describes the burning inferno of God's wrath against His enemies resulting in their consumption. His fiery Presence burns against those who are opposed to Him. And the day will come when Christ Jesus will return, and when He does, He will appear as a flaming fire to take vengeance on the wicked who do not know Him and do not obey Him (see 2 Thessalonians 1:8).

The Fire of God Consumed the Sacrifices

During Moses' time, God's people said they were afraid to come into God's Presence because they feared they would be consumed and die (see Deuteronomy 5:25-27). The Lord warned them as well because they were a "stiff-necked" people *not to* come into His Presence lest they be consumed (see Exodus 33:5). Their sin of rebellion would have caught fire like a patch of dry grass! Because God loved them, He kept them at a distance since He is a *consuming fire*. We have learned in earlier chapters that because of the death and resurrection of Jesus Christ, the final sacrifice for our sin has been paid, and we can now draw near to God. The curtain that separated the people from the Holy of Holies in the temple was torn from top to bottom when Jesus was put to death. This tearing of the curtain of separation was done by God the Father Himself because He wants us to come into His Presence, be near Him, and live. He sent His only begotten Son—the Lamb of God— slain from the foundation of the world to pay the penalty for our sin. Without the shedding of blood there is no forgiveness of sin the Bible tells us (see Hebrews 9:22); therefore, God paid the penalty Himself. Now, after accepting the sacrifice that He has provided, we can enter into His burning Presence and not be *literally consumed*. In other words, now we live—we really live—for now we are alive not only physically, mentally, and emotionally, but also *spiritually*. Lamentations 3:22 says, "Through the LORD's mercies we are not consumed, because His compassions fail not." In short, we live both physically and spiritually because of His great mercy. We have been saved—literally—by the sacrifice of His dear Son. The Father now looks upon the blood sacrifice of His Son and for the Christian who appropriates His sacrifice by faith, He sees it as enough to satisfy His burning wrath towards the evils of sin. That's why it is of the utmost importance to keep our sins confessed, repented of, and covered by His precious blood. In doing so, we draw near to God and invite His Presence into our lives. Our lives become a desired place for Him to dwell since there is no sin to repel Him and separate Him from us.

Laying our Lives on the Altar

Consumed means to be all gone, spent, with nothing remaining. When God's fire fell upon the sacrifice it licked it up; there was nothing left, it was all gone, it was spent, and it was consumed by the fire of His Presence. For example, 1 Kings 18:38 says, "Then the fire of the LORD fell and consumed the burnt sacrifice, and the wood and the stones and the dust, and it licked up the water that was in the trench." Also, Leviticus 9:24 says, "And fire came out from before the LORD and consumed the burnt offering and the fat on the altar. When all the people saw it, they shouted and fell on their faces." These verses tell us of the burning fire of the Lord and the results of that fire—it consumed everything—nothing was left. God's holy fire burned up the sacrifices of the Old Testament.

Yet God is calling us into His Presence. How then can we enter into His Presence and not be burned up? How is it that we can come into the Holy of Holies close to Him and live? It is by His mercy and by believing on our Savior, the Lord Jesus Christ, that we are not consumed; yet, He wants to consume us. God desires us to lay our lives upon His altar and become a sacrifice unto Him. Not in the sense of paying for our sin, no, Christ Jesus is the only one who qualified to be that sacrifice. He is the Lamb of God slain from the foundation of the world (see Revelation 13:8). We, His people, are to be *living sacrifices*, however. "I beseech you therefore, brethren, by the mercies of God, that you present your bodies a living sacrifice, holy, acceptable to God, which is your reasonable service (Romans 12:1). Our lives are not our own, we were bought with a price; therefore, we lay our lives on His altar as a *living sacrifice*, giving ourselves to Him wholly and completely.

The Cleansing and Purifying Fire

But who can endure the day of His coming?
And who can stand when He appears?
For He is like a refiner's fire
and like launderers' soap.

~ MALACHI 3:2 ~

We have some friends who own some land out west. Some of their land consists of fields where they plant special grasses. After some time weeds begin to get mixed in with the grass and cause an undesired blend. These weeds greatly reduce the quality of the harvest. To combat the problem, every few years they set the fields on fire. A trench is first dug up around the field to insure that the fire is contained to the field and does not spread, and then it is started ablaze. This fire is a cleansing fire used to purge the field of all the weeds and weed seed.

Our lives are like the field of the Lord. We need to be purged with the fire of His Presence to eliminate the ungodly weed seeds from growing up in our lives. The atmosphere of the world includes winds that blow in weed seed from the enemy's crops to contaminate the soil of our hearts and minds. The enemy may send a little bird to drop in a weed seed—a seed of thought from hell to be planted within our thoughts. If left undetected, this small seemingly unimportant, little seed grows into worthless, wild brush. Have you ever noticed what happens to a field that is left uncultivated? After a few short years, it is *full* of wild brush. We must submit ourselves to the fire of God's Presence, allowing Him to burn off all the unproductive growth.

Sometimes this purging of our spiritual fields happens through "fiery trials." "Beloved, do not think it strange concerning the fiery trial which is to try you, as though some strange thing happened to you; but rejoice to the extent that you partake of Christ's sufferings, that when His glory is revealed, you may also be glad with exceeding joy" (1 Peter

4:12-13). These fiery trials happen in order for us to exercise our free-will. It gives us a choice of burning for God or burning with the desires of our flesh, the wants of our eyes, and the pride of this life.

We will never know what is in us if we are not tested. Gold is purified in the fire. That is where all the dross is burned off; the dross is separated from the gold and skimmed off the top by the refiner. The more pure gold is the more valuable it is. Gold that is purified of all contaminates is 24 karat gold, the most valuable there is. As we allow the Spirit of the Lord to purge us through His refining fire, we become more and more refined. Therefore, we must allow ourselves to be purged by God's refining fire in the trials of life " that the genuineness of your faith, being much more precious than gold that perishes, though it is tested by fire, may be found to praise, honor, and glory at the revelation of Jesus Christ" (1 Peter 1:7). Indeed, as we trust in our Great Refiner, we shall go through the fire and not be burned up (see Isaiah 43:2). The process of God's refining fire can be uncomfortable, nevertheless, profitable. His burning processes will eliminate the ungodly dross in our lives.

It is only when we resist His processes that we become "burned." When we don't allow the dross to be removed from our lives, we desire to hang onto it; it is then that we are living a contaminated life, far beneath the purposes that He has designed for us. This is when we feel "burned." Have you ever said, "So and so burned me!"? Have you ever felt "burned" by someone? We all have. What is the answer? Let the dross be separated from you through God's refining process. Then give it to Him, the Refiner of your soul, and He will remove it from your life, purifying you in the process. The dross is what makes you feel bad anyways, so it is best to get rid of it. Dross is a contaminant. What does the dross of life consist of? In part, the dross consists of selfishness, pride, selfish ambition, greed, lust, covetousness, envy, hatred, and unforgiveness. What pollutes us is, in fact, sin in our fleshly nature. The book of Romans tells us that our fleshly nature wars against our spirits that have been made alive through Christ. These two natures war inside us. It is the fleshly nature that needs to be held to the flame of God's holy Presence. If we hold onto our dross-filled ways, we are polluting, contaminating, and poisoning our lives, and that poison then spills over into other people's lives as well. By surrendering them to God's refining fire, we are cleansed from them. It is then that we shine like gold and rise to His purpose.

Put the Coal to my Lips

My experience has been, the closer I get to the Lord, the more aware I am of my sinful nature. As we magnify Him, He magnifies us. Part of His magnifying us is that His gazing eyes see through us like a microscope, and He finds things that need refining within us. He sees our destiny, all the exploits that He wants to accomplish through us, and He wants to get us there, so He magnifies the imperfection in order to remove it from our hearts and lives.

God is holy, and He calls us to be holy too (see Leviticus 20:26; 1 Peter 1:15-16). He is always calling us upwards towards our potential and calling. Too many of us are living way beneath our callings. He calls us to live pure, holy lives. We must want it, too.

Prophet Isaiah was one who wanted it. He wanted it bad. Isaiah had a holy desire for God and to be in His Presence. His holy desire brought him closer to the Lord, and He came into a divine experience with the Almighty. He saw the Lord sitting on His throne with angelic beings called seraphim surrounding Him. Of whom he heard one cry out, in a voice that shook the whole house, "Holy, holy, holy is the LORD of hosts; the whole earth is full of His glory!" (Isaiah 6:3). There then was a manifestation of smoke that filled the house. Things were getting hot! Isaiah did not run from his experience; no, he was caught up in the Presence of the Lord, and he gave himself to the experience. He cried out to the Lord that He was a man of unclean lips and lived among others of unclean lips. In other words, he was made aware of his sinfulness, yet in that awareness, he did not run and hide. No, he yielded himself to the Holy One. A seraphim then flew to Isaiah with a live coal that was taken from the altar of God. He touched this coal to purify the lips of Isaiah while telling him that this coal had purged his sin and iniquity. After this fiery cleansing, Isaiah heard the Lord ask who would go for them (the Father, Son, and Holy Spirit). Now, being freshly cleansed by the fire of God's Holy Presence, Isaiah heard God's calling and was able to answer with, "Here am I, send me" (see Isaiah 6:1-8). Daily putting the "coal to our lips" keeps us purified and able to hear the call of God to go in His Name. Guilt caused by unrepented and unconfessed sin brings condemnation and causes us to feel unworthy so we do not hear the call to our daily purposes and plans that mark out the paths of our destinies. This is the sad state of many professed Christians; they are living far beneath their callings and destinies. We need God's holy fire in our lives to purify us, to cleanse us, and to prepare us for His call to service.

Consumed

Does God's fire consume us? While we die to self, we live for Him, so the answer is "yes", in a couple of senses. One sense is that His holy fire consumes our flesh. That is, our fleshly natures. I have heard it said that God loves the smell of burning flesh—meaning that He loves it when we allow His holy fire to burn off our fleshly desires and behaviors. In this sense we are living sacrifices. We hold ourselves to the fire of His Presence where our pride and selfish desires are burned off.

Secondly, we are consumed by His Presence in the sense of being fully devoted to Him. It is in this place that our very priorities change. No longer are the cares and worries of this world consuming our every thought. No longer are we caught up in selfish ambition and envy of others. No. Now He is our glorious obsession. He is our reason for living. He is behind every thought. He captivates our hearts, souls, and beings. This is why Mary sat at His feet. She was captivated by Him. Having found Him, there is no need to seek another. Priorities change. This is why the woman at the well left her water jar and went to tell others that she had found Him. Her priorities changed. No longer was she on a mission just to get water; she now found the living water and wanted to share her eternal drink with her friends. This is why the disciples, while on the road to Emmaus, constrained Him to continue on with them. There is something so consuming about His Presence. We want to be consumed with Him!

God is an all-consuming fire. He desires us to come close to Him so we can catch His fire. Because He is a consuming fire, when we come close to Him we catch fire too! Just like a building that is very close to another burning building catches fire, so too when you are close to the Lord, you also catch fire! It is then that we become like His burning bush upon His holy mountain; we are ablaze of fire, but we are not *literally* consumed. "And the Angel of the LORD appeared to him in a flame of fire from the midst of a bush. So he looked, and behold, the bush was burning with fire, but the bush was not consumed" (Exodus 3:2).

Even as God spoke through His burning bush to His servant Moses, while he was upon God's holy mountain, so too God will speak through us as we burn with His Presence and are filled with His words. God wants His fire to catch hold and spread to others. He wants us to set fire of His holy mountains in the earth, bringing restoration and reformation to the land! Joshua and Caleb said, "Give me the mountain!" What is your mountain? It is where God plants you and where He sends you. It is your home, your workplace, your church, your community. Set it ablaze for Him. We need to blaze a trail for others to follow and to light up the way for others with His Presence burning within us. This occurs as we become totally consumed with Him—obsessed with His Presence, purpose, and plans. It is then that His mountains are set ablaze, shining for Him. It is then that His holy fire spreads and burns off all the weeds, cleansing the land. God is waiting on us to catch His fire and be consumed with Him. As we are changed by His fiery Presence and spread His fire throughout the land, we change the world we live in.

Keepers of the Flame

My husband, Mike, and I have a small, old farmhouse in the country. There is nothing better than sitting around our woodstove on a cold winter's night enjoying its warmth and watching the flames that dance behind the glass door. To keep the home fires burning, we have found that we must both be "keepers of the flame." If we don't both take the responsibility of keeping the flame lit, it will invariably go out. Why? Because each one of us will mistakenly believe that the other one will tend to the flame. Likewise, we must each take responsibility to tend to our own spiritual flames. Not your spouse, nor your children, or even your pastor can be relied on to feed your internal flame. No, you must feed your own fire. Then you can burn brightly and allow your fire to "catch" to others.

If our woodstove flame is allowed to go out, it is much more difficult to restore. It can be done, of course, but is much more work. To restore the flame, we must first see if there are any hot ashes left. If there are, we can put some kindling on the hot ash and then fan the flame. If not, we must start by freshly lighting small leaves or paper and then adding the kindling to it. Once the flame is going, we put larger and larger pieces of wood upon it—feeding the fire into a burning source of heat and light again. Once it is a blazing fire, we need only to tend to the fire by feeding it with more wood regularly.

Our spiritual fires are much the same. We must tend to the fire within us by feeding it regularly with God's Word—both His written Word and His spoken word by spending time with Him. Of course, all spoken words we hear or sense, and all visions and pictures we believe He is showing us must be held to the written Word of God for accuracy. Nevertheless, it is His Word that burns within us. Prophet Jeremiah said that the Word of God was like a fire shut up in his bones, he could not help but speak it out (see Jeremiah 20:7-9). Even when he was being persecuted and mocked, and he wanted to hold back and speak no more in His Name, he could not hold back because the fire within him was so great. This is also why the Apostles, after the infilling of the Holy Spirit at Pentecost, could neither hold back when they were told to "speak no more in His Name" (see Acts 4:13-20). By not holding back, but speaking out of the fire within, God's fire spreads to others and He lights up their lives; therefore, it is imperative that we be keepers of the flame—His flame.

Re-igniting the Flame

There was a time in my life, many years ago, that I lost the fire. I was not "tending the flame." Oh, I went to church and kept up appearances, but my fire was barely flickering. The sense of His Presence was gone. Little compromises began to pile up in my heart and life until I found myself at a distance from the Lord relationally. When this happens we are not in the same place spiritually. That is why we call it "backslid." We have gone steps or paces away from the Lord. Sins of compromise put us at distance from Him; therefore, the anointing that comes from His Presence lifts from our lives. This is because He is holy; therefore, His tangible Presence lifts from our lives when our lives are yielded to sin. We need the breath of the Spirit to blow upon the embers of coal within us, so we allow His fire to cleanse and ignite us again. Then, as we give our lives back to Him as a sacrifice, we can be purged again by His Holy Fire and lit ablaze for Him again.

Sometimes it takes a while for us to begin to sense and feel His tangible Presence again. He, at times, tests us to see if we mean business or not. I recall when this happened to me, many years ago, that I found it hard to find my way back. I made a quality decision to read my Bible and to pray and worship Him, but I was not sensing or hearing Him. The devil began to taunt me by saying in my thoughts, "It will never be the same. It will never be the same." I heard this over and over again in my mind. I was battling the thought and losing. Then, one day, the Spirit of the Lord rose up within me and said, "That's right, it never will be the same ... it will be better!" I rejoiced with that word! And the enemy fled! And so it was, God gave me the grace to finish the test. I disciplined myself to study the Word of God and pray and worship, and His tangible, precious Presence came upon my life once again. My life was re-lit for Him. We must never take His Presence for granted. If we find ourselves at a distance from His Presence, we must turn away from our sinful path of self and take steps towards Him, as we pray as David did: "Do not cast me away from Your presence, and take not Your Holy Spirit from me" (Psalm 51:11).

Are you in a place where your fire has gone out? Is your flame but a flicker? Do you desire His flame to consume you afresh? Or, do you desire Him to consume you more and more? Then say this prayer with me:

Prayer

Lord, I lay myself upon Your holy altar as a living sacrifice. Forgive me for not tending to my fire. I confess every sin of thought and deed that I have committed and allowed to put out the fire of God in my life. Forgive me, I pray, and rekindle the flame of God in my heart and life. Fire of God come and burn in me today. Burn off all the dross in my life that I may shine as pure gold. Burn off all the wood, hay, and stubble from my life, heart, and ministry. Put the coal to my lips, I pray, that I may be purified and hear Your fresh call to me. May my fleshly nature be consumed in Your fiery Presence. Burn within me, I pray. May Your Word burn in my bosom, and may Your fire within me catch hold to others as I follow Your pillar of fire—Your Presence—in Jesus' Name. Amen.

CHAPTER 13

Changed in His Presence

But we all, with unveiled face, beholding as
in a mirror the glory of the Lord, are being
transformed into the same image from glory
to glory, just as by the Spirit of the Lord.

~ 2 CORINTHIANS 3:18 ~

CHANGES ARE A part of life that we all experience. Some changes are pleasant while others are resisted. I am a creature of habit and, for the most part, find that I don't like much change. When things are the same, they are predictable and I feel safe. However, sometimes things get boring and then I find that I need a "change." Sometimes a new outfit or hairstyle will do the trick. I tend to take a long time in prayer before making big changes in my life. Sudden changes can take all of us all by surprise. An accident or a death in the family can be a very troubling and painful change. The weather changes continually and cannot always be predicted. I live in western New York where the weather is always changing. I always make sure to have a jacket in the car with me because the weather may change several times before the day is over. Our world is constantly changing around us. We go through political changes, cultural changes, occupational changes, just to name a few. Ladies go through what we call the "change of life," although men are not without changes while aging.

We many times make promises to ourselves and others at the beginning of the year that we will change. We call them "New Year's resolutions." It is then that we try to make some desired changes in our lives such as: to lose weight, stop smoking, or change some other difficult habit in our lives. These changes are much more difficult than a mere change of clothing. Some changes are good and others are bad, some are easy while others are difficult, but one thing is for sure ... the world we live in is constantly changing.

In the beginning God created us in His image and likeness (see Genesis 1:27). After the fall of mankind, our image changed. Sin changed our appearance and our actions. The need for change for each and every one of God's created persons was indeed made clear. We all need to be changed. Every person needs to be made brand new. "Therefore, if anyone is in Christ, he is a new creation; old things have passed away; behold, all things have become new" (2 Corinthians 5:17). He makes all things new. He changes us from the inside out! And as we behold His glorious Presence we are changed from glory to glory (see 2 Corinthians 3:18).

God brings these much needed changes into our lives as we surrender our lives to Him. No New Years' resolution, no

change of mind, no new agenda will bring the spiritual changes that we need in our hearts and lives. Many people desire to
change but lack the power to do so. It is only by calling upon
Jesus and receiving the power that He has that our lives can
be truly changed. We must press in to see Him, to have Him
in our presence, to be in His Presence, to hear His Word. He
is knocking upon the door of our hearts, but we must let Him
in. And then we must allow ourselves to be changed—changed
in His Presence. The Bible is full of true stories of those who
desired to be in Jesus' Presence and allowed Him to change
them. One such person was the man Zacchaeus.

Zacchaeus

Zacchaeus was a tax collector who heard that Jesus was going
to be passing through town. He most likely heard about Jesus
and had a desire to see Him for himself. He wanted to catch a
look at Him as He was passing through his area, much like we
would do if a celebrity or person of importance were coming
to our area (see Luke 19:1-10).

The crowd, however, blocked Zacchaeus's view. Perhaps
you have desired to get a closer look at Jesus, or to get closer to
Him relationally, but other people got in your way. People can
block our view of Jesus if we let them. They can overshadow
Him with their views, their behaviors, and sometimes their
misguided theology. If we allow people to get in the way, we
will miss our personal encounter with Him. We must not be
content with other people's thoughts and ideas about Jesus, or

even their inspiring testimonies. Rather, let their testimonies motivate you to come closer to Jesus to encounter Him on a deeper level. And, if others have a limited view of Him, know that you don't have to be limited, but can truly experience Him fully.

Zacchaeus did not allow others to block His view of Jesus; he found a way to see Him for himself. Zacchaeus located a sycamore tree and running ahead, he climbed it so as to obtain a good view of Jesus. If we are going to see Jesus more clearly, we must come up higher. We must raise ourselves up out of our daily routines and away from the crowds of distractions. Raising ourselves up out of the mobs of mundane, mainstream monotony takes effort but, as we do, our flesh is subdued and our spirits stretched. The reward is like the Mount of Transfiguration where we experience God and see Him more clearly than ever. No other story or picture painted by another can compare to that glory—the glory of being in His Presence.

Not only did Zacchaeus not let others get in his way, but neither did he allow them to put him down or make little of him. You see, the Scriptures tell us that Zacchaeus was a man of small stature, but he did not allow that to stop him from seeing Jesus. Nor did he think less of himself because of his size. He did not allow feelings of unworthiness or insignificance to hinder him from seizing the opportunity to see the Son of God as he passed through his town. If we are going to see Jesus for who He is and gaze upon His awesome glory, we must not see ourselves as insignificant and unworthy to do so. Rather, we must realize that the reason Jesus came is to seek and save the lost and to draw us unto Himself.

Zacchaeus positioned himself correctly. He came up high enough to see Jesus clearly. Not only did he see Jesus, but the most extraordinary thing happened—Jesus saw him too! When Jesus came to the place where Zacchaeus was, He yelled out to him to come down because He was coming over to his house for dinner! Wow, what an opportunity! So, Zacchaeus quickly scurried down the tree to greet his divine dinner guest and take him home with him.

The same invitation is made to us as well. When we position ourselves correctly and align ourselves with the purposes and plans of God, we are in the right place at the right time, and our hearts are open for the entrance of the Spirit of God. We then find ourselves touched by His Presence.

Be Changed

This divine encounter changed this tax collector's life forever. Tax collectors were loathed by the people because they often were dishonest, keeping some of the collected monies for themselves. But after his encounter with Jesus, Zacchaeus *was changed* for he said that if he took anything from anyone wrongfully, he would restore it fourfold! Also, he gave half of all his goods to the poor! Zacchaeus allowed himself to be personally challenged while in the Presence of the Lord. He then chose to align himself with Christ. He allowed the glory of God to rub off on him and to surrender his selfish ways. Zacchaeus was changed in His Presence.

Some mistakenly say that we are always changed in His Presence. Not true. If that were true then everyone that went to an anointed church service would be changed. We all know that, sadly, is not the case. Even during times of great revival services and great outpouring of God's Spirit, not everyone is changed. The fact is … heart change is our choice. Either we submit to Him, or we don't. It is that simple. Take, for example, the Biblical account of the rich, young ruler. He also was in Christ's Presence. Yet after he asked the Lord what he must do to be saved, he received an undesirable challenge: The Lord knew that he had great riches and, more importantly, these great riches *had him*. So the Lord challenged him to give his riches to the poor. The Scripture tells us that this young, rich ruler went away grieved. Why? He was unwilling to let go of what had a hold on him. He was unwilling to put Christ first in his heart and life. He was unwilling to *change*. This rich, young ruler stands in stark contrast to the willing tax collector, Zacchaeus. That is why people can be in an anointed church service where the Word is preached with fire, and the Spirit of the Lord is present and moving during a worship service. People are touched and may even go to the altar, or even go down under the power of God, and yet, leave *unchanged*. Our free will is a factor. We must align ourselves with His Word, His will, and His way by yielding to Him in obedience. This obedience to Him changes our reactions, or mindsets, and our habits.

I wish the fruit of the Spirit would come upon us by osmosis, but it does not. The fruit of the Spirit must be grown. These fruits are love, joy, peace, patience, kindness, goodness, faithfulness, gentleness, and self-control (see Galatians 5:22-23). Though we may have an encounter with God, we must *allow* ourselves to be changed by His Presence. It is a daily surrender which is indeed moment by moment. Unfortunately, a bad decision can be made in an instant and can cause us to lose the sense of His Presence. We need to be close to Him and yielded to Him every moment of every day by making godly choices in order to bring and keep the changes He is requiring in our lives. This requires a daily dying to selfish desires but, as we do, His Presence and anointing increase in our lives. It is then that His Holy Spirit is *truly* welcomed. It is then that He comes upon us and we are changed.

Softened in His Presence

We are all being molded and shaped into the vessels that He desires. However, before a lump of clay can be molded and change shape, it must first be softened. A hard mass of dried up clay is like concrete—unmovable. It, therefore, will remain unchanged. The Israelites, while wandering through the wilderness, were said of the Lord to be "stiff-necked." That means they were hard and set in their ways, unyielding, and resistant to His Presence. All humans have that nature within them that is contrary to God. He wants to change us. He wants to soften us. "I will give you a new heart and put a new spirit within you; I will take the heart of stone out of your flesh and give you a heart of flesh" (Ezekiel 36:26). Although this initial change occurs upon our regeneration at our rebirth, it is also an ongoing process, for we are changed from glory to glory.

Glory to Glory

Changing into His image and likeness is a metamorphosis. After Paul exhorted the church to become living sacrifices to God, he then said to be transformed or changed by the renewing of our minds to the Word of God. We are changed by taking His Words of life into ourselves, chewing on them, and making them the standard to live our lives by. When we do this, we believe His Words and, having believed, we change our thoughts to His thoughts. After changing our thoughts to His thoughts, we then change our behavior to His behavior. It is then that our lives begin to take on a different look.

We go from glory to glory. Just as we travel to the upstairs of a house one step at a time, and the one step takes us to meet the next, so also, taking one glorious step with the Lord brings us to the next. And, before you know it, you are at a whole new level in Him! There are even elevator moments, when we take one great step of faith in obedience to Him, and God moves us quickly to the next floor. He rewards us with His precious Presence! He anoints us with the oil that only comes from His Spirit upon our lives.

Walking with Him daily takes us into His glory realm. There are mountaintop experiences awaiting each of us. No doubt while on our mount of transfiguration we will want to set up a tent and stay there. Nevertheless, we will need to come down to go out into the valleys and tell of His wonders, so others will desire to take their pilgrimage as well. However, we do not go alone; He goes with us. He not only is in us, but like Moses when he descended from the mount of the Lord (see Exodus 34:29), His increased glory is seen or sensed upon our lives.

Glorious Change

After progressively changing our hearts, minds, and lives, we then can begin to change our corner of the world. We are to become world changers! That is the stuff reformation is made of. God is calling us to reform the way we live our lives as His body and church. He wants us to be overcomers and world changers. Having overcome our own weaknesses and shortcomings, we then can teach others how to do so as well. We must be moving forward as a people and as a church, hastening the day of our Lord by changing our world. We pray, "Your Kingdom come, Your will be done on earth as it is in heaven." But we must realize that He desires to do that *through us*. We must make sure our actions are being such as to bring godly change into our neighboring communities and, therefore, usher in His Presence.

"And let the whole earth be filled with His glory. Amen and Amen" (Psalm 72:19).

Beholding His Glory

"But we all, with unveiled face, beholding as in a mirror the glory of the Lord, are being transformed into the same image from glory to glory, just as by the Spirit of the Lord." (2 Corinthians 3:18). Now, while we are on earth prior to His final return, our gazing upon Him is much like looking through an old time window glass. Those old glass windows were rippled and a bit cloudy and, therefore, the images seen through them were not "crystal clear." You had to look intently to see clearly. Likewise, we must look intently and purposely into His written Word and press into the tangible Presence of the Lord through our praise and worship in order to encounter Him. His glory does shine forth, however, and is able to pierce through the darkness of our cloudiest day. By keeping His image and likeness before us, we are able to catch glimpses of His magnificent Presence. As we gaze upon His beauty, we behold His glory.

That glorious image must then be held onto. Much like an artist sees what he wants to paint and then holds that image in his mind's eye in order to duplicate it on canvas, so also we must hold onto His image in our inner eye and cherish Him in our hearts in order to duplicate His ways in our lives. By doing so, we allow His Spirit to have full expression through us. Only then can we make His mark upon the hearts and lives of others. He makes all things beautiful in time—through us. Each day is, in fact, like a piece of blank canvas waiting for the stroke of God's hand upon it. He is teaching us to paint by taking our hand in His and painting His world through us. Behold His glory! Hold onto His image, and place your hand in His. Color your world with His beauty. By doing so you will be changing the world you live in.

Prayer

Lord Jesus, I press in past the crowds of others to gaze upon Your beauty. I determine not to let others hold me back from seeing You more clearly and from having You come more intimately into my life. Speak to me through Your written Word and through prayer. Show me Your desire to be expressed in my daily life. Change me to be more like You every day. I desire to be softened in Your Presence, so You can mold me into Your desire. May Your Kingdom come, and Your will be done on earth as it is in Heaven. Use me to be a world changer and to bring Your Kingdom into the lives and hearts of others. Express Yourself through me I pray. Amen.

CHAPTER 14

§

Carriers of His Presence

And let them make me a sanctuary, that I may
dwell among them.

~ Exodus 25:8 ~

In Old Testament times God traveled with His covenant
people. He led them with the cloud of His Presence—the pillar of cloud by day and fire by night. His Presence went before them, and they followed Him. He so desired to be with
His people that He placed His very Presence upon the Ark of
the Covenant—the gold covered box that was transported by
the Levites wherever they went. He then gave instructions to
Moses, while he was with Him upon the Mount, of how to
construct the Tabernacle. The Tabernacle would hold the Ark
of His Presence and would be placed in the Holy of Holies—a
dwelling place behind a curtain where only the High Priest
could enter, and then only once per year to make sacrifice.
After Jesus came and made the final sacrifice by dying on
the cross to pay our death penalty for our sins, the curtain

that was in the Temple was torn from top to bottom by God Himself, showing that Jesus opened the way into His marvelous Presence once and for all. We now can enter in behind the veil by the blood of the Lamb—Jesus Christ the Son. We are now all able to enter into His Presence. The way was opened by the Way—Jesus.

During King David's time, the Ark of the Covenant was held for a period of time in what is called the Tabernacle of David. It was held there until his son Solomon built the Temple. The unique thing about the Tabernacle of David is that it had no veil or curtain. It was a one room tent that housed the Ark of the Covenant. Also, worship was going on twenty-four hours a day. There are Scriptures that speak of God restoring this Tabernacle:

On that day I will raise up
the tabernacle of David, which has fallen down,
and repair its damages;
I will raise up its ruins,
and rebuild it as in the days of old.

~ Amos 9:11 ~

Acts 15:16 also speaks of the Lord restoring the Tabernacle of David. Notice, it is the Tabernacle of David that God is restoring not the Tabernacle of Moses. What's the difference? The difference is that in the Tabernacle of David there was no veil separating the people from the Presence of the Lord.

David's tabernacle was a foreshadow of what was to come. It was speaking of the day when there would be no need for separation from God's Presence because Jesus, the final sacrificial Lamb, was slain. Now, by having our sins atoned for by His blood, we can receive His forgiveness and cleansing and be free from our sin. Now we can enter into His Presence. This is the tabernacle that God is restoring to His people—a place of nearness of His Presence and a place of continual worship.

His Temple

When Jesus walked the earth he was quoted as saying that He would tear down the temple and rebuild it in three days (see Matthew 26:61; Mark 14:58; and John 2:19). He was, in fact, not speaking of the temple made with human hands but rather His body. He died and was buried and rose from the grave on the third day. He ascended into Heaven and sits at the right hand of the Father. He poured out His Holy Spirit. Believers are now His temple. "Do you not know that you are the temple of God and that the Spirit of God dwells in you?" (1 Corinthians 3:16). Yes, now He dwells in us; therefore, we are His temple. Mission accomplished! Now we can commune with Him in the sanctuary of our very own hearts. Now, as we draw near in our hearts, His Spirit is stirred which, in turn, stirs our spirits. As His Spirit is aroused, our spirits are aroused for His purposes.

There is no reason for sin to separate us, for He bore our sins in His body on the tree of the cross. To allow sin and guilt to separate us from Him is indeed a shame, for He died to abolish that! Yet, sin is the number one reason that people, even His called out ones, distance themselves from Him. To continue to hang onto sin, or the shame of past sin is, in fact, a slap across His face. We must surrender to Him daily, lay our sin at His feet in repentance, and press in to His Presence. Then we can come boldly to His throne to find grace in our time of need. Being filled with His Spirit is what makes us His sanctuary. Our very hearts become His abode—His home.

Built *Together* the House of the Lord

There are those who say that they have the Lord so they don't need to go to church anymore. They feel that they can worship God in their own way and, therefore, are not in need of going to church. While it is true that His Spirit dwells within His believers, and we can indeed be filled with His Spirit, yet we are *built together* the house of the Lord. "You also, as living stones, are being built up a spiritual house, a holy priesthood, to offer up spiritual sacrifices acceptable to God through Jesus Christ" (1 Peter 2:5). We are each a living stone that is built together—fitted together for Him. "Now, therefore, you are no longer strangers and foreigners, but fellow citizens with the saints and members of the household of God, having been built on the foundation of the apostles and prophets, Jesus Christ Himself being the chief cornerstone" (Ephesians 2:19-20). We are all members of His household, and He Himself is the cornerstone. Therefore, we need to come together as the house of the Lord.

We are built together a house of the Lord, and we are built upon the foundation of the Apostles and Prophets. The Apostles and Prophets are not somehow cemented into the foundation as a memorial; no, their offices also were resurrected by the Lord Jesus Christ! He has restored all five-fold offices (Apostle, Prophet, Pastor, Evangelist, Teacher) back to the church for the equipping and perfecting of it. These headship offices equip the saints, and impart anointing for the work of ministry. "Till we all come to the unity of the faith and of the knowledge of the Son of God, to a perfect man, to the measure of the stature of the fullness of Christ" (Ephesians 4:13). The Lord is currently maturing His saints and bringing them into unity. That cannot be done if we allow ourselves to be separate and forsake the gathering of ourselves together, which, unfortunately, is the habit of some (see Hebrews 10:25). We need each other. We are built *together* the house of the Lord.

Mobile Home

Even as God traveled with His people in the Old Testament times, He also travels with us. No longer is He appearing as a pillar of cloud or fire before us; nevertheless, He still travels with us. Now, He is within His believers' hearts. He dwells in our very midst. We are, in fact, God's mobile home. Because we are mobile, we can travel. And where we go, He goes. Yes, we want to be led by His Spirit to the places that He desires us to go, but He never really leaves us. Even if we travel outside His will, He is still with us because He is everywhere; however, we can then lose the sense of His tangible, precious Presence. We want our wills to be lined up with Him, to stay in step with Him, to go where He would have us go, and to practice abiding in His Presence. He has the road map; we are to follow His directions. If we find ourselves "off course," we must stop and ask Him for His Divine directions.

Because we are His mobile home, we carry His Presence wherever we go. We need to be more and more aware of this fact. We need to learn to cultivate His Presence in our lives and hearts in order to usher others in. It is like we hold the key to the Most Holy Place. We can open the door for others to enter into His Presence and experience His greatness. I have seen movies where in order to get into a secret room, you have to put your thumbprint on a screen that reads it, and it then lets you enter in. We all, in a similar way, must have the thumbprint of Christ Jesus dipped in His blood that was poured out for us all, applied by faith in order to enter in. We enter the Holy of Holies by applying the blood of the Lamb to our lives by faith. Those who call upon Him are saved. He meets them where they are at, and He ministers to their needs. Not only can we lead the way into His Presence, but we can bring His Presence to others and meet them where they are at. Wherever we go, there are people to reach out to and share our faith with. Wherever we go, there are lost and hurting people. We—His people, His saints—are His mobile home! Remembering this fact will keep us on task and mindful to be aware of His Presence.

After saying that the Lord was restoring the Tabernacle of David the Scripture goes on to tell us the reason, "*So that* the rest of mankind may seek the LORD, even all the Gentiles who are called by My name, says the LORD who does all these things" (Acts 15:17, emphasis mine). Our purpose is to reveal Him to others, so they also seek after Him and find Him.

Your Purpose

Carrying His Presence is your divine purpose in life. It makes no difference what place you find yourself in, you are called to carry His Presence. Understanding this mission in life and being remindful of it moment by moment will be life changing, for if we are on task with this mission, we will not be caught up in self and the worldliness that surrounds us. If we remember what we are here for—to carry Him to others—we will be doing our purpose "on purpose." In other words, we must be purposeful about our purpose and stay focused on that purpose. Having this attitude is life changing, both for you and others. The Apostles were purpose minded. Apostle Paul, for example, "purposed" in the Spirit that he would go to Jerusalem, and that after being there that he would go to Rome for Christ (see Acts 19:21). Not only did he purpose in his spirit, but he purposed in the Spirit. This means that he was in communion with the Holy Spirit about where he was to go next. Being purpose minded means we are praying throughout our day about where to go and what to say. It means we are always looking for opportunities to share Christ and His Kingdom with others. It is being mindful of others' needs around us and being willing to minister to those needs. This is being purpose minded "on purpose."

Called To Carry

In preparation for His Triumphal Entry, on what we now celebrate as Palm Sunday, Jesus sent His disciples to fetch a young donkey colt for His entrance into Jerusalem. This was an inauguration of sorts. Usually, when a king was inaugurated they rode into the city on a high stepping and highly decorated horse. Jesus, however, chose a humble donkey for His ride into the city.

This donkey was unbroken—that is, it was never ridden before. Yet, that donkey was chosen for such a time as this—to carry the Presence of our Lord and Savior into the city. That donkey, though he was not broken, yielded to the Lord and carried Him without fault. We, too, are like that young donkey. The Scriptures have several verses that compare our human nature to that of a donkey's. The book of Job (11:12), for example, says that man is born as a wild donkey colt! The reason is our fleshly human nature. The book of Romans tells us that our carnal nature is contrary to God. It is that fleshly nature that wants to rise up and rule and war against our spirit-man. We are made of up of three parts: our spirit, soul, and body, and our soul is divided up into three parts as well: our mind, will, and emotions. It is the selfishness of our soul and our flesh that wars against our spirit-man that wants to please God. It is that stubborn human nature that wants to kick up its heels and run about doing its own thing. We can be as stubborn as a mule and kick against the pricks as Paul did before his conversion. We can dig our heels in and resist yielding because we want our own way. Some other verses that speak of the comparison of our human nature to a donkey are Jeremiah 2:24 and Hosea 8:9. We can tend to get one thing on our minds that appeals to our flesh and go after it, all the while bucking against the Lord's directions. As a result, we buck off His Presence.

Despite our fleshly human nature, God has need of us. He has chosen us, just like He chose that young donkey colt. He wants us to carry His Presence. He wants us to yield to His seat of authority in our lives and carry Him into our world.

Be Loosed!

Before this chosen donkey could rise to the occasion of carrying the Presence of the Almighty, it first needed to be loosed. Jesus told His disciples to go and get the donkey colt; however, it was tied up at the place where two roads met and needed to be loosed. We too need to be loosed from things that hold us back and bind us up. Many times this happens at the crossroads of life. We get stuck in our ways and hesitate from going down the road that God is pointing out to us. We must make our decision firm to follow Him, regardless of the cost. Choose His road. Choose His way. Choose His direction.

His disciples loosed the colt from its bondage. We too need to be loosened from the things that bind us in order to carry His Presence. Here is an acronym for the word "loose" to represent things we need to be loosed from:

> **L**ove of money
> **O**ffenses (unforgiveness)
> **O**verly concerned (worry, anxiety)
> **S**oul ties (people, places, things, idols)
> **E**go (self)

Love of Money – As long as we are caught up in the love of money we will be bound to it. The Scriptures tell us that where our treasure is, there is our heart (see Luke 12:34). When we are held captive by the love of money we are, in fact, practicing idolatry.

When I was employed in my last occupation, I had become unknowingly ensnared by a love of money. The spirit of mammon had gotten its claws into me. This can happen to us while being totally unaware and can especially happen if we are in an occupation that is goal oriented and money driven. With all this focus on "getting the money" we can unknowingly become enslaved to a spirit of mammon. The Lord called me out of that place and into full time ministry with Him. The truth is … we cannot serve both God and mammon (see Matthew 6:24). We must serve God and He will take care of the rest. The bottom line is … God will take care of you. Trust Him. "But seek first the kingdom of God and His righteousness, and all these things shall be added to you" (Matthew 6:33).

Offenses – When we hold on to offenses, we are binding up ourselves and others. That spirit of offense becomes ensnared around us holding us back from the freedom we could have in Christ Jesus. We must forgive. When Jesus hung on the cross, after being beaten, spat upon, tormented, mocked, and nailed to a cross, He prayed to His heavenly Father and said, "Father, forgive them, for they do not know what they do" (Luke 23:34). We must follow His example and forgive others. When we do, not only do we loose others to be forgiven, but we also loose ourselves from the bondage of offense.

Overly concerned – When I say overly concerned, I am speaking of becoming tied up in the concerns of life. We are bound by worry. Worry is a fear of what has not yet occurred, and may never occur. It is a lack of faith and trust in our Lord and Savior for our future or future of our loved ones. Sure, we all have responsibilities and concerns, but we must learn that after we do what we are responsible for, to cast those cares upon the Lord and trust Him to take care of them. "Be anxious for nothing, but in everything by prayer and supplication, with thanksgiving, let your requests be made known to God; and the peace of God, which surpasses all understanding, will guard your hearts and minds through Christ Jesus" (Philippians 4:6-7). Give God your concerns in prayer and leave them with Him and you will be loosed from worry.

Soul ties – When we put other people or other things before God our souls become tied to them. This is, in fact, a sin of idolatry. We have held that person or thing at such a high regard that they or it has become a snare to us. We have com-promised our faith for it and have become ensnared *by it*. The Scriptures tell us, "He who loves father or mother more than Me is not worthy of Me. And he who loves son or daughter more than Me is not worthy of Me" (Matthew 10:37). This means we are not to put anyone before the Lord. God must be first in our lives; after Him come spouses and children. As you give the Lord those relationships and trust Him with them, and as you make a decision to turn from compromise and to put Him first by obeying Him, you will be loosed.

Ego – when I speak of ego I am speaking of self. Many of us are too tied up in ourselves. This boils down to selfishness and pride. We must humble ourselves and learn to put others first. When we begin to live for God and lovingly serve His people, then we find fulfillment. We cannot do that while we are caught up in our own affairs. Volunteering at church and in the community by giving of our time, talents, and gifting, will loose us to be free from the selfish ties that bind us.

All of these things can bind us up and cause us to lose the sense of His Presence. Confess them before the Lord and renounce them in Jesus' Name. By doing so you break the tie that binds you.
There is yet another thing that we can look to Jesus to be loosed from, and that is a spirit of infirmity. There are times when we are literally bound up by such a spirit. Luke 13:10-13 says, "Now Jesus was teaching in one of the synagogues on the Sabbath. And behold, there was a woman who had a spirit of infirmity eighteen years, and was bent over and could in no way

raise herself up. But when Jesus saw her, He called her to Him and said to her, 'Woman you are loosed from your infirmity.' And He laid His hands on her, and immediately she was made straight, and glorified God." Ask Jesus, your Divine Physician, to loose you from the spirit of infirmity, and give God the glory for His grace. Finding His grace in the time of our need gives us a testimony to share with others. Our testimony will encourage others to seek Him for His healing virtue as well.

We can also lay hands on the sick and pray for them to be loosened from a spirit of infirmity, while asking for God's healing grace to be poured out in their lives. In short, we must be loosed from anything that holds us back from serving Him!

Carry On and Cross Over

Christ Jesus has chosen you and loosed you for the honor of carrying His Presence forward into places that He desires you to go. With that in mind, we carry on while staying focused on our purpose of carrying His Presence within our hearts and upon our lives. We stay focused on fellowshipping with Him, and we stand ready to minister His Presence to the others around us.

When the Israelites crossed over the Jordan, they carried the Ark of His Presence. Crossing over the Jordan was a landmark crossing for it was then that they entered into their promised land. Finally they had arrived, while carrying His Presence, and yet, it was His Presence that carried them. He brought them to the Promised Land. It was like the crossing of the Red Sea when they came out of Egypt in that it was a miraculous crossing. The waters parted! Only this time it was different. When they left Egypt, their leader Moses raised his staff and the Red Sea parted. This time, they carried the Ark of His Presence, and the waters of the Jordan parted! It was the Presence of God that was being carried by the church of that day that brought this miraculous parting!

Today, you and I are the carriers of the Presence of God, and we are crossing over into our promised lands. We all have ground to take for God. We all have flood waters that need to part. We all have our mission fields; we all have our mountains to conquer in His Name. It cannot happen without carrying His Presence. He anoints us to go forth and to conquer in His Name. He anoints us to possess.

Possess

This is the time to possess! It is not the time to stand back and be a spectator. God wants us to go forth in His Name and carry His Presence. Know your gifts, know your calling, and know your place— where He is calling you.

> Arise, shine;
> for your light has come!
> And the glory of the LORD is risen upon
> you.

~ Isaiah 60:1 ~

Arise and shine for His Spirit is arising. He wants you to shine Him forth to the world around you. He wants you to know your mission and take Him there. He will give you the grace, power, and strategy to take the ground for Him. His Presence will anoint you.

As we take ground for Him, the enemy loses his foothold. Remember, the Promised Land was the land that ten of the twelve spies of Moses had years before announced as unattainable since it was filled with giants. Those giants did not leave in the meantime. No, they stayed until they were dispossessed by God's people. We must know our authority in Him and take that authority in the spirit-realm by telling the enemy spirits to go in Jesus' Name. We then occupy. We occupy like an army until Jesus' return. That is our calling—to occupy. We set up His Kingdom by carrying His Presence and operating in His authority and Kingdom principles of grace. It is not by our power or our might, but by His Spirit that we overcome. That means we do not fight in the natural, but in the spirit. Love is our greatest weapon. Love your enemies, and do good to those who hurt you. At the same time, put on the whole armor of God and bind up the enemy spirits behind them in Jesus' Name, for we do not wrestle against mere flesh and blood but the enemy spirits operating behind the scene (see Ephesians 6:12; Matthew 16:19). This is our spiritual warfare. This is how we overcome. Praise Him all the while. Praise is one of our greatest weapons. We overcome a little at a time. One step at a time we conquer in His Name.

It is time to possess. His Presence will cause the waters to part. His Presence will usher in the miraculous. His Presence will displace the enemy spirits. Our job is to carry Him forth and carry Him over. Our job is to listen to His commands and obey His instructions. As you do, He will go before you and the waters will part, opening the way before you into your portion of the Promised Land. You have an inheritance. We must carry on; carry on in His Presence. Carry His Presence.

His Presence Awaits

While it is important to spend time waiting on His Presence, basking in His Presence, yet He is waiting on our presence. He is waiting for us, longing for us, to join up with His Spirit for the journeys that await. He is our Guide. He desires for us to call upon Him and team up with Him for the journey ahead. Call upon Him. Join up afresh with His Spirit to carry Him forth.

No longer does He need a gold box to carry Him forth. No longer does He need a Tabernacle or an elaborate Temple building to dwell within. He has you. He has us—the corporate church—the body of Christ, to be filled with His Spirit and to be His temple. This mindset makes every day an adventure and every task worth doing.

His Presence brings hope. His Presence brings faith. His Presence brings peace. His Presence brings protection. His Presence brings power. His Presence brings the miraculous. And His Presence brings change. Go in His Presence and change your world.

Closing Prayer

Lord, I want to carry Your Presence forth into the land that You are sending me to. You have the roadmap. You are my Guide. Direct me and lead me. I want to carry You as You carry me. Be the strength in my life. Be the light that shines out of me. Give me Your love and fruits to share with those I meet along life's way. Give me the boldness to conquer in Your Name and the wisdom to do so. May Your Spirit empower me for service, and may Your Presence be felt and longed for by those I encounter. Change my world one glorious step at a time as I am faithful to carry Your Presence into the world I live in. In Jesus' Precious Name I pray. Amen.

"The grace of the Lord Jesus Christ, and the love of God, and the communion of the Holy Spirit be with you all, Amen" (2 Corinthians 13:14).

Would you like Kathy to minister at your church, conference, or training center?
You may contact her at:
Kathy Wypij
303 Route 39 W
Arcade, NY 14009
716-392-8442
Kathyskeystothekingdom@gmail.com
Kathy Wypij Ministries.com

To purchase more copies of this book
In His Presence: A Handbook for Coming into the Presence of God
Or Kathy's first book *The Keys to the Kingdom: Keys Revealed to
Unlock Heaven in Your Corner of the Earth*
Contact her directly or go to
Amazon.com